"Gorick Ng uses skills honed at Harvard on how to approach any complex problem and simply break it down into its component parts. This is a highly readable and essential guide for every young person who wants to succeed."

—**DAVID CAREY**, former Global President and Chairman, Hearst Magazines

"I had a massive inferiority complex as a first-generation college student from a liberal arts background. *The Unspoken Rules* helped me turn that anxiety into confidence."

—**CHRISTINA L.**, business development intern, media

"Working at a startup, it was easy to lose sight of what I really wanted because we were building so quickly. *The Unspoken Rules* helped me define my professional goals and position myself for a promotion I didn't know I could have."

—**WINSTON H.**, chief of staff, health care

"School taught me how to code and debug but not how to turn managers and coworkers into allies. Thanks to *The Unspoken Rules*, I went from not having anyone to lean on to building lifelong friends and mentors."

—**PRIYA R.**, software engineer, finance

"I felt lost while remote onboarding to my first full-time job, which had no HR and coworkers who were too busy to train me. *The Unspoken Rules* taught me how to be proactive, ask the right questions, and convince my manager that I am ready for more important responsibilities."

—**ANDRÉ M.**, political staffer, government

"After reading *The Unspoken Rules*, I realized why I didn't get a return offer in my previous internship. Now, two months into a new job, my boss has even told me that she has never seen this level of ownership and professionalism from a recent grad before!"

—**HONG L.**, marketing analyst, nonprofit

"Switching careers is stressful, especially when all of your colleagues have years of experience. *The Unspoken Rules* gave me a framework for earning others' trust from day one. I went from feeling like an impostor to being recognized as a quick learner and effective teammate."

—EMMANUEL C., human resources, biotechnology

"In my first job, I was so concerned about making the perfect comment that I was always quiet in meetings with senior partners. *The Unspoken Rules* helped me find the confidence to speak up, so I'm now an active contributor in investment committee meetings."

—MARIA G., investor, private equity

"*The Unspoken Rules* isn't only for when you have a boss. Knowing how to prioritize, keep the team on the same page, and communicate efficiently is even more important when you don't have anyone looking over you."

—EUGENIO D., cofounder, startup

"You need to do more than show up, lecture, and grade assignments to succeed as a teacher. You need other teachers to respect you and your department head to trust you. How do you build a reputation like that? No one teaches you this—not until *The Unspoken Rules*."

—ARIEL F., high school teacher

"*The Unspoken Rules* completely changed how I work with my principal investigator. No more all-nighters—now I'm setting clear boundaries, 'managing up,' and deciding when to follow instructions and when to think for myself."

—RICHARD Z., graduate researcher, academia

"When I began my career, I thought that putting in the hours and winning cases would make me stand out. *The Unspoken Rules* not only helped me realize the importance of relationship building in promotion decisions but also gave me the tools and confidence to put myself out there."

—KATHRYN R., law student

"Succeeding in tech is all about figuring out what you need to do—and then rallying people with different priorities around that goal. No one teaches you how to deal with ambiguity and manage yourself and other people. *The Unspoken Rules* does."

—HASSAN A., product manager, technology

THE
UNSPOKEN
RULES

THE
UNSPOKEN
RULES

SECRETS TO
STARTING YOUR
CAREER OFF RIGHT

GORICK NG

HARVARD BUSINESS REVIEW PRESS
BOSTON, MASSACHUSETTS

Copyright 2021 Gorick Ng
All rights reserved
Printed in the United States of America

10 9 8 7 6 5 4 3

No part of this publication may be reproduced, stored in or introduced into a retrieval system, or transmitted, in any form, or by any means (electronic, mechanical, photocopying, recording, or otherwise), without the prior permission of the publisher. Requests for permission should be directed to permissions@harvardbusiness.org, or mailed to Permissions, Harvard Business School Publishing, 60 Harvard Way, Boston, Massachusetts 02163.

The web addresses referenced in this book were live and correct at the time of the book's publication but may be subject to change.

Library of Congress Cataloging-in-Publication Data
   Names: Ng, Gorick, author.
   Title: The unspoken rules : secrets to starting your career off right / Gorick Ng.
   Description: Boston, MA : Harvard Business Review Press, [2021] | Includes index.
   Identifiers: LCCN 2020047844 (print) | LCCN 2020047845 (ebook) | ISBN 9781647820442
     (hardcover) | ISBN 9781647820459 (ebook)
   Subjects: LCSH: Career development—Handbooks, manuals, etc. | Success in business—
     Handbooks, manuals, etc.
   Classification: LCC HF5549.5.C35 N55 2021 (print) | LCC HF5549.5.C35 (ebook) | DDC 650.1—dc23
   LC record available at https://lccn.loc.gov/2020047844
   LC ebook record available at https://lccn.loc.gov/2020047845

ISBN: 978-1-64782-044-2
eISBN: 978-1-64782-045-9

The paper used in this publication meets the requirements of the American National Standard for Permanence of Paper for Publications and Documents in Libraries and Archives Z39.48-1992.

For those who dream.

And for Mom, who taught me the unspoken rule of paying it forward.

CONTENTS

SECRETS TO
GETTING THE JOB DONE

SECRETS TO
GETTING ALONG WITH EVERYONE

SECRETS TO
GETTING AHEAD

PREFACE

It was 2:30 a.m. and I was still in the office, frantically trying to fix a broken Excel spreadsheet that was to be presented to a client in six hours. Was this what the job posting had meant by "dynamic" and "fast-paced environment"?

Then, ding! A notification popped up on my laptop. My manager was asking me to hurry up.

Ding! Another message.

Ding!

I sent the updated spreadsheet to my manager. Ten minutes later, he still hadn't replied.

"Gorick," said a voice behind me. I sprang off my chair and turned around. It was my manager. "Let's work through this together," he said. We sat side by side for another two hours. He took over my laptop, and I looked over his shoulder, desperately trying to keep my eyelids from shutting.

My manager pointed to a cell. "Why are we dividing these numbers?"

I leaned over and squinted. "I'm not sure."

He sighed. That night felt like surgery without anesthesia. As my head throbbed, I wondered: How did I end up in this situation?

The answer came in a performance evaluation ten months into my job: *Gorick needs to fully own his work, including going through the painstaking preparation of taking over someone's Excel project.* When I read my review, I was puzzled. "Own his work?" Sure, my manager told me to "own the Excel analysis," but I thought that meant I was responsible for keeping the master (the main and most up-to-date) file. What did it mean to own my work? My manager had said I did a good job in the end. *I* thought I did a good job. What was I missing?

It was knowledge of the unspoken rules—certain ways of doing things that managers expect but don't explain and that top performers do but don't realize. Knowing how to navigate the unspoken rules is essential to career success. The problem? They aren't taught in school. Instead, they are passed down from parent to child and from mentor to mentee, making for an unlevel playing field between insiders and outsiders.

How do I know? Because I was one of the outsiders.

My mother used to say that getting ahead is all about hard work. My mother was wrong: It's not just about putting your head down, staying quiet, and letting your efforts speak for themselves. Hard work is only the price of admission to the game of career building. To survive and thrive in this game, you need something more. You need to know the rules of the game.

When I was fourteen, my single mother was laid off from her job at a sewing machine factory. She had never written a résumé or a cover letter before. Neither had I, but as the only child and the only one in the house who knew how to use a computer, I stepped up. I spent lunches learning to write résumés, afternoons at the public library searching for housekeeping and laundry attendant jobs, and evenings submitting hundreds of job applications for my mom. On weekends, I helped my mom scrub strangers' bathrooms to make ends meet.

Months went by. Every one of our applications went unanswered. We had spent hours polishing each cover letter, so to not hear back at all was devastating. We felt stuck. As a last-ditch effort, my mom applied for a government grant and returned to school—her first time in nearly forty years—to become an early childhood assistant. After earning her certificate, my mom secured several child care jobs that she held until retirement. We survived, but barely.

Since then, I kept wondering: How could someone as hardworking as my mom have such a hard time getting back on her feet? And how could I, despite my googling, not help her? The answer came years later, when I was in high school. During a community service event I met an older student from another school named Sandy, who was in the middle of applying to America's top colleges. It hadn't occurred to me that I could ·

apply to these schools; I hadn't even heard of many of them. Through Sandy, I learned that there was more to the admissions process than the instructions on colleges' websites. I learned that it was not enough to simply ask for a reference letter from my teachers—I had to share a list of accomplishments I'd like them to showcase. I learned that my GPA and standardized test scores would only get me so far—my extracurriculars and personal story would matter just as much. These strategies worked. I became the first person in my family to attend college—at Harvard University.

At the time, I thought the unspoken rules were behind me. Little did I know they had only just begun.

I was returning to my dorm one night during sophomore year when several classmates hurried past me. I was wearing jeans and a hoodie. They were wearing suits. In class the next day I overheard whispers about an invite-only reception that had been organized by a company from a recent career fair. I had walked by the company's table but hadn't spoken with anyone. After all, I was under the impression that companies didn't hire sophomores. These other sophomores not only pitched themselves to the recruiters but also got friends of friends to put in a good word for them. I emerged from the career fair with a brochure and free branded water bottle. They emerged with job interviews.

Weeks later, I was sitting in class while these other students were out of town attending "sell weekend," a time when college students were invited to companies' headquarters to be wined and dined after receiving their job offers. Suddenly, I understood why my mom and I had struggled. We had been blindly applying to jobs online, not realizing that people who succeeded had built relationships behind the scenes.

I sprang into action. I befriended older students and did what they did. The unspoken rules worked. I landed the types of jobs that the insiders had gotten: a junior summer internship in investment banking at Credit Suisse and a full-time job in management consulting at Boston Consulting Group (BCG). But as I learned later from my performance evaluation, getting in was one thing. Surviving was another.

This time, I knew better. I started talking to coworkers and friends about their jobs, their frustrations, their performance reviews. What began as one-off venting sessions quickly became daily conversations outside of work. To my surprise, it didn't matter if someone worked at a startup, a law firm, a hospital, or a school. We were all struggling with the same issues.

Before long, I expanded my reach. I started cold emailing managers and asking them to rant to me about their teams. Soon I was video chatting with strangers halfway around the world and listening to company leaders complain behind closed doors. Our conversations revolved around three key questions:

- What are the most common mistakes people make at work?

- What would you do differently if you could redo the first years of your career?

- What separates top performers from mediocre ones?

Nearly five years later, I've asked these questions to over five hundred people—CEOs, managers, and early-career professionals across geographies, industries, and job types. These people helped me see what I could have done better in my career. And thanks to their wisdom and kindness, life got better. It took another six months, but I went from almost crying at my desk to presenting in meetings. I went from feeling micromanaged to managing my manager.

Since then, I've tried to pay it forward by sharing with others what I wish someone had shared with me. I became a career adviser at Harvard College and the University of Massachusetts Boston and have coached hundreds of students and early-career professionals across the United States and Canada. However, for every person I've met who was hungry to succeed but didn't know how to do it, there are countless others I will never get to meet. That is why I wrote this guide—to pull back the curtain on the secrets of high performers that take years to figure out alone.

In this book we will walk through the unspoken rules that underpin successful careers, step by step. These rules aren't relevant only for your first job, internship, or apprenticeship; they're relevant for any role in any industry, whether you're a longtime employee or just stepping back into the workforce. This guide is about more than how to *start* your career; it's about how to *navigate* your career—and *succeed* in it.

One note before we dive in: don't worry about reading this book from cover to cover. There are a lot of strategies, tactics, and talking points to take in. I hope you'll refer back to certain chapters and sections as your career progresses, or as you hit roadblocks. Your career is a journey, and nailing the secrets to getting ahead is too.

The unspoken rules are now in your hands. Learn them and make them work for you.

Gorick Ng
www.gorick.com

THE
UNSPOKEN
RULES

INTRODUCTION

The Unspoken Rules

B elow are the unspoken rules of starting your career off right. They are not complete, however, without the secrets that will help you *live* by them. In the rest of the book we will discuss how to align your behavior with these rules so that you can be successful and make an impact. Keep the rules in mind as you read this book. Treat them like a pair of lenses you put on to analyze and navigate the world.

Reject, embrace, or bend the rules

Figure out which rules make sense (or don't), are worth questioning (or aren't), or compromise your values (or don't). Then decide for yourself whether—and when—you should reject, embrace, or bend the rules. Be aware of the difference between what's right and what aligns with your manager's preferences. Learn when a piece of feedback is productive and should be accepted—and when it isn't and should be discreetly ignored. Find allies.

See the big picture

When joining a new team, research what the team does, what its objectives are, whom it serves, what it's been up to recently, who its competitors are, who the most important people are, and how your role will help the team and organization achieve their goals. When taking on a new assignment, understand the broader objective, what success looks like, and how your work fits into the big picture. Stay up to date with what's happening in your team, company, and industry.

Do—and show—your homework

When you have a question, avoid immediately pulling others aside. Look through your emails and files and search online first. If you can't find the answer, bundle and escalate: bundle your questions and then ask a co-worker at your level for help, followed by the next most junior or relevant person, and so forth. Explain where your question is coming from, and share what you've done to figure things out yourself. Share what you know before asking about what you don't know.

Think like an owner

Imagine that you own the entire project and don't have anyone to go to for help. What would you do to solve the problem? Imagine you are in charge of your company. How would you help it achieve its goals? Be proactive: Is no one saying hello? Then say hello. Is no one sharing information? Then ask for information. Is no one giving you work? Then ask for work. Give others something to react to. Bring solutions, not problems. Take control of your career.

Show you want to learn and help

When you're new to a team or project, people expect you to ask questions ("learner mode"). Over time, people expect you to know what's going on and to make thoughtful contributions ("leader mode"). Know if you are in learner mode or leader mode and act accordingly. Treat "Any questions?" not as a "yes" or "no" question, but as a "yes" question. Always have a question or a point of view. When in doubt, ask, "How can I be helpful?"

Know your internal and external narratives

Know why you do what you do. When introducing yourself, talk about your past, present, and future: share what you've done, what you're working on, and, if relevant, what you're trying to achieve. Consider framing your personal story as a Hero's Journey: what sparked your interest, what you've done, what brings you here today, and what you hope to achieve. When giving a status update, talk about what you've done, followed by what you still have to do.

Know your context and your audience

Are you more extroverted or introverted? More experienced or less? In the majority or minority? Be mindful of—and manage—the biases that others may have toward you. And know your audience: What concepts are they familiar or unfamiliar with? How do they like to learn new information? What do they want to hear? When speaking or writing, personalize your message to your listener or reader. Find the most appropriate person at the most appropriate time.

Mirror others

In unfamiliar settings, compare how you come across and how others come across. Find people you respect and can relate to, observe how they behave, dress, write, and speak, and adopt elements that are authentic to you. Mirror the urgency and seriousness of the people you are working with. Show more urgency and seriousness when interacting with someone who has leverage over you. When in doubt, let others go first.

Manage your intent and impact

When interacting with others, understand that your intent (how you mean to come across) may not be the same as your impact (how you actually come across). Clarify what people can misinterpret about you: explain any behavior or actions that can be seen in a negative light to prevent others from assuming the worst. If your intent can be interpreted in multiple ways, don't rely on emails or instant messages; opt for a conversation instead.

Send the right signals

Be intentional about what others can see, hear, smell, and feel from you. Be mindful of cultural norms around eye contact, smiling, responding promptly, and single-tasking. When others give you instructions or advice, take notes in front of them. Do what you say you will do (or proactively explain yourself). Be mindful of when and how you arrive, speak up, send emails, and ask for help. When in doubt, show up early.

Think multiple steps ahead

Learn what your manager might ask of you—and have it ready. Know what issues your manager might face—and offer a solution. Before submitting your work or entering a meeting, brainstorm what you might be asked and have a response ready. When making decisions, consider the second- and third-order implications. When others tell you to do something, think multiple steps ahead: Do their directions make sense? Might their idea cause issues for others?

Work backward from the end goal

Understand what you are trying to achieve, then work backward, mapping out all the steps and deadlines between you and the end goal. Make sure you are clear on what you need to do, how you need to do it, and by when. Ask colleagues and superiors, "When would it make sense to check in?" Repeat back what you think you heard before walking away. Then, constantly assess whether what you are doing is getting you closer to the end goal.

Save others time and stress

Before asking people to help you, list the steps they will need to take and remove as many of them as possible. When scheduling meetings, offer your availability in the other person's time zone. Be deliberate and clear with your subject lines, key takeaways, and calls to action. Leave nothing ambiguous. Try to explain your idea in three points or fewer. Before starting a discussion, provide background information so everyone knows what's going on.

Recognize patterns

Avoid making the same mistakes twice. Avoid making others tell you something twice. And avoid asking the same questions twice; if you must, acknowledge it or try asking someone else first. Look for patterns: if your manager always asks for X, be ready with X before they ask next time. Find ways of working that help you work more productively. Solve problems at their root cause. Make sure your patterns of behavior align with how you want others to see you.

Prioritize what's urgent and what's important

Prioritize what has the earliest deadline, involves the most people, causes the most anxiety, gets harder over time, is central to your role, or matters most to those who matter. Know that what's important to you may not be what's important to other people, and vice versa. Know what people are looking for (and not looking for) given the time you have. Focus on what people will scrutinize. Split tasks into have-to-dos and nice-to-dos—and do the have-to-do tasks first.

Read between the people

Be mindful of invisible chains of command, swimlanes (who does what and when), comfort zones, and loyalties. Know who reports to whom, who is responsible for what, and who has leverage (power) over whom. Identify who the influencers are. Be aware of behavior that people find acceptable and unacceptable. Keep people consulted and informed. Make others look and feel good. Know when to step up and when you may be overstepping.

Engage, ask, repeat

Look for excuses to connect with people. Engage with what others have to say—listen, absorb, think. Then make a comment or ask an open-ended question. Let people finish speaking. Balance your speaking time. Once you've interacted with someone, greet them when you encounter them again. Send thank you emails. Ask how things are going. Offer to help. Share relevant news. Broker introductions. Look for and call out commonalities between you and other people.

Own up

Ask for feedback if you aren't sure how well you are doing. Try asking, "What should I start doing, stop doing, and keep doing?" Or, "Am I on track?" Be mindful of when you should apologize and admit that you were wrong and when you should defend yourself. If you make a mistake, be prepared to apologize, explain what happened, offer a plan to mitigate the impact or fix the problem, and explain how you will avoid making the same mistake again.

Push gently

When asking for help, frame it as a request, not a command. Give others a chance to decline. When you disagree with someone, use "I wonder . . . ," "What if . . . ," or "Pushing back . . ." to frame it as constructive feedback rather than as criticism. Before proposing an idea, try to understand whether a similar idea has been proposed before and, if so, why it failed. When you're new and have little leverage, frame ideas as questions like "Have we considered . . . ?"

Show performance and potential

Know that you are being evaluated based on both your performance (how effective you are in your current role) and your potential (how effective you might be in your next role). To show your potential, claim an un-claimed swimlane: do what hasn't been done, fix what hasn't been fixed, bridge what hasn't been bridged, know what others don't know, and share what hasn't been shared. Don't let potential go unrecognized. Ask for what you want—and deserve.

Observe the people around you at work. Notice how those who get ahead have mastered most, if not all, of these unspoken rules—and how those who struggle repeatedly stumble with at least one or more of these same rules.

How can you apply these unspoken rules to your own career? That's where the rest of this book comes in.

The Three Cs

Competence, Commitment, Compatibility

Before we dive in, let's discuss a framework that will carry us through the entire book: the Three Cs—competence, commitment, and compatibility. The minute you step into a new role is the minute your managers, coworkers, and clients will ask themselves three questions:

"Can you do the job well?" (Are you competent?)

"Are you excited to be here?" (Are you committed?)

"Do you get along with us?" (Are you compatible?)

Your job is to convince your managers, coworkers, and clients to answer "Yes!" to all three questions. Prove that you are competent, and people will want to offer you more important responsibilities. Prove that you are committed, and people will want to invest in you. Prove that you are compatible, and people will want to work with you. Demonstrate all three Cs as seen in figure 1-1, and you'll maximize your chances of building trust, unlocking opportunity, and getting closer to achieving your career goals.

FIGURE 1-1

The Three Cs: Competence, commitment, and compatibility

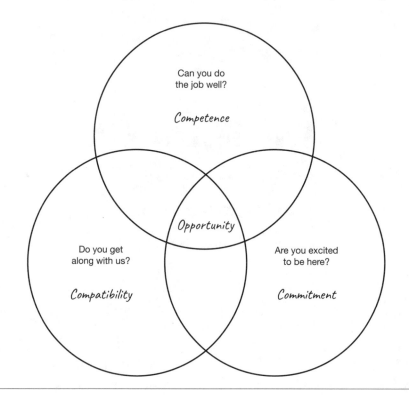

It's not enough to show one or two of the Three Cs. You need all three. Otherwise, people won't trust you with important assignments, won't feel like you are worth their time and investment, or won't want to spend time with you (figure 1-2).

Let's begin by defining each C and discussing why they can be so challenging—and yet so important—to navigate.

Competence

Competence means you can do your job fully, accurately, and promptly without needing to be micromanaged—and without making others look

FIGURE 1-2

How people think about your Three Cs

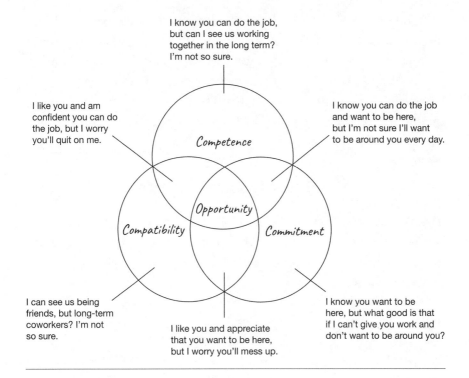

bad. This means not undershooting to the point of looking clueless and not overshooting to the point of looking overbearing.

A college student I met had landed a remote market research internship at a startup during the school year. Midway through her semester, she got busy with her classes. She hadn't started the latest research project she was supposed to have already finished. Her manager kept calling and emailing, but she didn't pick up the phone or reply for over a week.

She was planning to catch up on her work after her midterms. But before she could catch up, she was fired—for not communicating and, as a result, looking clueless.

Another time, a recent graduate of a teacher training program had been hired by a high school. In conversations with others in his department, he kept saying, "In my training we learned about 5E Lesson Planning. Did you know about this? It's better than the old way of lesson planning, and students like it more." The veteran teachers crossed their arms and shot him a "get away from me" look. Before long, he acquired a reputation for being a naive know-it-all from people seeing him as overbearing.

The challenge with competence

True competence can be difficult to measure. It's easy if you're a baker or coder; one simply has to taste your cake or test your code. But for many jobs—where much of your day is spent interacting with people—measuring competence isn't easy at all.

In the absence of clearly measurable outputs, managers often rely on inputs—like how much progress it looks like you are making on a project, how confidently you speak in meetings, and how well you promote yourself. It's no surprise, then, that the people who get promoted or who get the highest-profile assignments aren't always the most competent—even within organizations that claim to be meritocracies. Your actual competence still matters, but, as we'll discuss later in this guide, your perceived competence can be just as important.

Commitment

Commitment means you are fully present and eager to help your team achieve its goals—but not so eager that you put others on the defensive. This means not undershooting to the point of looking apathetic and not overshooting to the point of looking threatening.

A summer camp counselor was accused of being lazy by the camp director despite working hard and taking on extra tasks. One of his fellow counselors pulled him aside and helped him see that the issue wasn't his lack of effort; it was his lack of enthusiasm. He looked mellow and often had his phone out. His fellow counselors, on the other hand, behaved like they were in a musical about peppy camp counselors. Over the following weeks, this counselor threw on a smile, walked faster, and added a spring to his step. To his surprise, the director started taking him seriously—all because he no longer looked apathetic.

Another time, a college student had gotten an internship at an investment bank. Anytime he got his own work done early, he'd start doing his teammates' work without asking. He sometimes even corrected his manager in front of higher-ups. In the end, he was one of two interns who didn't receive a full-time job offer—all from being threatening.

The challenge with commitment

The struggle with commitment is the same as the struggle with competence: perception and reality don't always align. Just because you *are* committed doesn't mean people *perceive* you to be committed. Sometimes, little actions like showing up late, looking away on video chat, not volunteering for tasks, not speaking up enough, or not replying to emails as quickly as your coworkers do can be enough to cast doubt on how committed you are.

It's hard to tell what's real and what's perceived. It's even harder if you work in a system that mistakes perception for reality and where people prioritize style over substance. This is not to say that you should want to stay in your job forever, though. Your first job likely won't be your last job. People get that. Your interests and goals can change. People get that too. But people do expect a certain level of perceived commitment, which we will discuss further in this book.

Compatibility

Compatibility means you make others comfortable and eager to be around you—without coming across as inauthentic or trying too hard. This means not undershooting to the point of looking passive and not overshooting to the point of looking like a poser.

One time, a cashier at a movie theater was told by her manager to be more of a "team player." She was confused. She always showed up to work on time and dealt with customers politely. But it wasn't enough because she hardly smiled and didn't make small talk with her manager as her coworkers did. She didn't pass her probation period—all because she looked passive and withdrawn.

Another time, a recent graduate of an American MBA program joined a corporate strategy team at an energy company in Asia. One day, he attended a supplier presentation with some senior coworkers. At the end of the presentation, the vendor asked, "Any questions?" The room went silent. Not realizing that his coworkers were following a cultural norm of waiting for the most senior person to speak first, he blurted, "Well, if none of you have questions, *I've* got a question." His coworkers all rolled their eyes—and saw him as a poser.

The challenge with compatibility

What's challenging about compatibility is that it depends on whom you're with and what norms and unconscious biases they have. People like people who are similar to themselves, so they tend to hire, hang around, and promote those who look like, talk like, and have the same backgrounds and interests as they do.[1] And because these biases can be unconscious, it's easy for even well-meaning people to treat others unfairly without realizing it. People might claim that someone is not a "cultural fit" when they are really judging the person's clothes, accent, mannerisms, body weight, hobbies, or any other element of the person's identity.[2]

If you are joining a team where everyone looks like you, sounds like you, behaves like you, and has experiences and worldviews similar to yours, then you may never think twice about your identity. But if you are joining a team where people are different from you, whether in terms of race, ethnicity, socioeconomic background, gender, sex, sexual orientation, dis/ability, religion, age, degree of introversion or extroversion, or other characteristics, then your identity can influence not only how others judge your Three Cs but also how you see yourself.

When I first entered the workplace, self-doubt set in almost immediately. Being of Asian descent and defying the "model minority" myth that all Asians must be timid and good at math, I couldn't keep up with the many data projects I was being assigned over my non-Asian coworkers. As someone who was never taught how to send professional emails, I couldn't keep up with my coworkers' rapid-fire messages because I kept having to edit and re-edit my writing. And as a first-generation, low-income college student, I couldn't contribute to my coworkers' small talk about their childhoods because my mother couldn't afford the same sports equipment, music lessons, or vacations when I was growing up.

In the language of the Three Cs, I was struggling with my *competence* because I was making mistakes that people didn't expect me to make. I was struggling with my *commitment* because I wasn't responding to emails as quickly as my coworkers. I was struggling with my *compatibility* because I wasn't contributing to my coworkers' conversations. The fact that I came from an elite undergraduate institution didn't help. The expectation was that I'd be wealthy and would know what I was doing. Not wanting to expose myself as an impostor, I kept my mouth shut.

The workplace is not a level playing field. For some, competence is expected; for others, incompetence is expected. For some, commitment is assumed; for others, commitment is questioned. For some, compatibility is effortless; for others, compatibility is tiresome. Different people will start off in different locations in the Venn diagram of the Three Cs— and have different distances to travel to get to the center.

A Black woman engineer told me about the pressure she faced to hide her natural Afro in work environments that saw straight hair as the only standard for professionalism. A transgender finance professional told me about their experience of not getting invited to their coworkers' afterwork parties and their managers' reluctance to put them in front of clients. A Latina woman working in politics told me about how she was accused of being dumb yet bossy whenever she spoke up in meetings with all older men.

A Muslim woman in the energy industry told me about the constant dilemma she faced of deciding how to navigate lunch meetings and client dinners when she was fasting for the holy month of Ramadan. A Black man on a team of all white women in the beauty section of a department store told me he had been informed that he wasn't a "culture fit" because he didn't show up to his coworkers' after-work socials at a bar. A white woman who worked in accounting in New York City told me about her fears of being labeled a dumb jock because she was a former college athlete or as racist or uneducated because she came from a small, blue-collar farming community.

Sikh men, Muslim women, and Jewish men working in the corporate and nonprofit worlds told me about the unspoken pressure they faced to conform to the dress code of their coworkers who were not used to seeing turbans, hijabs, or kippahs. A Black man working in finance told me about his struggle with "casual Fridays," when he'd feel pressure to look casual enough for his coworkers, but professional enough to be taken seriously by clients—and not be racially profiled on his way home from work. A startup executive with a physical disability told me about his struggle to overcome the perception that he was less competent than his peers. And women everywhere have told me about all the times they'd share an idea, only to have a man say the exact same thing and take all the credit.

These stories are more than individual experiences. They are examples of patterns that have been formally studied and verified scientifically. It's disappointing to hear, but the following statements are true: Women often walk a tightrope of needing to be both likable (so, not too "masculine") and competent (so, not too "feminine"). Black people tend to be more closely monitored at work than white people are. And people with easy-to-pronounce names tend to be evaluated more positively than people with difficult-to-pronounce names.[3]

Is this fair? No. Do we need a better system? Yes. Might we have a better system by the time you start your job? If only.

Sometimes we can use no other words than "racism," "sexism," "classism," "ableism," "ageism," "heterosexism," "lookism," and all the other "isms" to explain why some people fail to reach their full potential in the workplace. But until we achieve justice and equality for all, I want you to learn from those who've gone through the system the hard way.

As difficult as it may be to navigate differences, the journey is worth it. After all, without differences, you would not be unique. You would not be *you*. Your uniqueness is not a liability. It is an asset. In fact, it is a superpower waiting to be unleashed.

The Black woman engineer I interviewed went on to recruit more Black women to the engineering profession. The transgender finance professional went on to help their company establish more-inclusive policies. The Muslim woman went on to create a community of Muslim professionals in her city. These individuals not only found their superpowers; they used their superpowers to lift others up. You can do the same.

We'll be on this journey together, guided by the Three Cs. By the end of this book, you will have not only the vocabulary to diagnose what's happening around you but also the tools to become the professional that you have the potential to be.

Let's begin!

Remember This

- Your challenge as a newbie is to convince your managers, coworkers, and clients to answer "Yes!" to three questions: Can you do the job well? Are you excited to be here? Do you get along with us?

- You convince your managers and coworkers to answer "Yes!" by demonstrating the Three Cs of competence, commitment, and compatibility.

- To show competence is to show that you can get the job done fully, accurately, and promptly without needing to be micromanaged.

- To show commitment is to show that you are fully present and eager to help the team achieve its goals.

- To show compatibility is to make others comfortable and eager to be around you.

SECRETS TO

GETTING
STARTED

Think, "Let's Give This a Shot!"

The first step to showing up in a new job is getting into the right mindset. Over the course of a new job (or any job) you will come across countless opportunities—to meet new people, to take on more important responsibilities, to stretch yourself. These opportunities will present themselves like road signs whizzing by as you're driving down a highway.

Know This

- Opportunities will come your way all the time.

- Career success depends on your ability to identify and seize the right opportunities.

- The secret ingredient? The mindset of "Let's give this a shot."

But these opportunities are nothing more than that—opportunities. They aren't valuable in and of themselves. They are valuable only if you seize them. Whether a road sign becomes anything more than a slice of painted metal stuck on a pole is up to you, the driver, to decide. It takes a special type of driver to recognize—and seize—an opportunity. What separates the driver who acts on the sign from all the others who let the opportunity pass them by? A mindset of "Who knows? Let's give this a shot."

I learned this lesson from Annie (not her real name; all names and some details have been changed in the stories for privacy), a recent college grad who was hired at an oil and gas company. She was part of a program in which she rotated to a different team each year for her first three years at the firm. A week before her first day at the company, Annie received an email from HR listing all the teams that were hiring, along with a survey allowing her to rank the available options. She was placed in her third-choice team. Although Annie enjoyed her first rotation at the start, she started getting restless by the end of six months. She didn't enjoy the work and couldn't relate to any of the higher-ups, so she had a hard time imagining a future with the department. She also wasn't looking forward to her next placement. Most of the other teams didn't interest her, and the one that did wasn't even listed as an option on the preference survey from HR.

During a monthly check-in with her company-assigned "buddy," Annie wondered what to do.

"Why don't you talk to the head of the team you want to join?" her buddy said.

"Am I allowed to do that?" Annie asked. "Isn't that weird?"

"Why would it be weird?" her buddy replied. "The survey doesn't make the decision—people do. If the head of the team wants you, why wouldn't you get the position? And besides, what do you think everyone else is doing? Waiting around? They're likely doing this too."

Immediately after the meeting, Annie drafted an email, reviewed it with her buddy, and sent it to the senior vice president (SVP) of the team she wanted to join:

Subject: Joining your team for next rotation

Hi Chiderah,

My name is Annie and I am a marketing analyst currently on rotation with the natural gas liquids team. Hope this email finds you well.

I wanted to see if there might be an opportunity for me to join your strategic partnerships team for my next rotation starting in July. I was inspired by your department's recent promo video and would love to help you increase your university partnerships. (In university I helped a professor with his grant proposals, so I have experience navigating the academic side of things.)

Might you have 15 minutes to discuss further? I am available at the following times (CT):

- Tue 2/4: before 11 a.m.

- Wed 2/5: before 1 p.m., after 3 p.m.

- Thu 2/6: after 10 a.m.

- Fri 2/7: any time

Looking forward to hearing from you,

Annie

After hitting Send, Annie kept refreshing her inbox, hoping for a reply. After nothing but radio silence for two weeks, Annie sent a follow-up email:

Hi Chiderah,

I wanted to follow up on my email below regarding my interest in joining your team. Might you have a few minutes to chat? My updated availability is as follows (CT):

- Tue 2/18: any time

- Wed 2/19: after 11 a.m.

- Thu 2/20: any time

- Fri 2/21: before 1 p.m., after 2 p.m.

Best,

Annie

Annie waited another week. But still—no response.

Why isn't she responding to me? Annie wondered. *Is she busy? Does she not have any open positions? Does she not think I'm a good fit? Or, did she simply forget to reply?*

Annie searched for the SVP on the company's instant messenger. Her status was green. She was online. *Could I just message her?* Annie thought. *No, that's too much.*

She leaned back in her chair and saw a quote she had stuck above her monitor: "Do the thing you fear most and the death of fear is certain." *You know what? Let's give this a shot. What's the worst that could happen? She says no?* Annie typed her message in a separate document to prevent herself from accidentally clicking Send:

Hi Chiderah—Please forgive the message out of the blue, but I am interested in joining your team and was wondering if you'd have time to chat. I sent you a few emails, but didn't hear back, so I guessed that maybe I wasn't a fit, but I wanted to make sure.

Annie pasted the message into her chat window, reread the message several times, held her breath—and clicked Send. Minutes later, Annie received a call. It was Chiderah, the SVP.

"Hi Annie, Chiderah here. I thought it'd be easier to call. Sorry, I don't have a role."

Annie felt herself deflating into her chair but tried to keep an upbeat tone. Chiderah began talking about being one of the few women executives at the company and supporting young women like Annie in advocating for what they wanted. At the end of the call, Chiderah asked if Annie would be interested in joining a book club for women at the company that she was starting. Annie was still disappointed in the lack of a role but agreed anyway. *Who knows?* she thought. *Maybe I'll learn something.*

A week later, Annie received an email from Chiderah about the book club. Noticing that six other women at the company were CC'd on the email, Annie looked them up on the company's intranet and on LinkedIn. They were all executives. Annie was the youngest person on the email by at least fifteen years. Chiderah ended her email with a question:

> What do you all think?

A week went by and no one responded.

Maybe I can help, Annie thought. Chiderah's email didn't contain any details on how the book club would work, so Annie replied-all with a plan:

> Chiderah—I'm happy to help. Here's a quick plan I drafted.
> What do you all think?

Chiderah responded after only a few minutes:

> Love it. Let's do it.

A month later, Annie and Chiderah officially launched the company's first women's book club. Immediately, Annie went from not knowing any senior leaders at the company to knowing a dozen of them. After the second book club meeting, Chiderah emailed Annie.

> I haven't forgotten about your rotation. Just put a note in your preference survey saying that you'd like to be on my team. I'll speak with HR.

Fast forward and Annie became the first person to be placed on Chiderah's team for a rotation.

If opportunities are like signs on the side of a road, then Annie not only saw the signs but also relentlessly pursued them. Had she not looked beyond the list of available rotation options, asked her buddy for advice, contacted the SVP, followed up, embraced the SVP's opportunity, and stepped up when no one else would—all while keeping a smile on her face—she probably would have ended up at her third choice again.

When I heard Annie's story, I was amazed by her drive and tenacity in going after what she wanted. I wanted to know how she did it. And, just as important, how did she find the confidence to do it?

Annie: "Oh, I was really insecure the entire time. I was the only person in my cohort from my college. I was the only woman, too. I had to constantly remind myself that I'm worthy of being here."

Gorick: "How did you do that?"

Annie: "I gave myself credit for everything I've done to get to where I am: I picked a tough major in college. I had leadership roles on campus. I worked part-time to pay for school. I was the only person from my college to be hired by this company. Surely these experiences count for something?"

Gorick: "They do! But most of us don't just wake up one day and declare, 'All right, I'm going to turn on my confidence today!' Where did all of this confidence come from?"

Annie: "I got a C on my first essay in college. I was devastated. But I knew I couldn't let it go like that—not with so much of college still ahead of me. So, I brought my essay to my professor and said, 'Tell me everything I'm doing wrong.' It took time to improve, but by the end of the semester I had the highest grade in the class. I learned that you can grow a lot by growing a little—the important thing is to just start trying. I brought this mindset with me to the workplace."

Gorick: "But isn't it scary to put yourself out there like that?"

Annie: "Oh yes! That's why I had that quote on my wall: 'Do the thing you fear most and the death of fear is certain.' I need to constantly remind myself—the scarier something seems, the better it probably is for me. But if you don't put yourself out there, you won't grow. It's as simple as that."

My conversation with Annie taught me three lessons.

Where you start off does not have to determine where you end up. Whether it was the C she got on her essay or the feeling of being an outsider in her job, Annie didn't look back except to give herself credit for everything she had accomplished to date. She looked forward. And forward was exactly where she went.

If you do the bare minimum, you will get the bare minimum. The role Annie wanted didn't exist on the preference survey, but that didn't mean it *couldn't* exist. In her words, "You can't wait around for others to decide your future. You need to create opportunities for yourself." If you don't ask for it, you won't get it.

The worst thing that could happen is probably not that bad. If the worst-case scenario is the other person says "no," your fear is really a fear of judgment—not a fear of danger. Leave it to other people to tell you "no." Don't limit yourself before you've even given yourself a chance.

Don't let the fact that you have less experience than others on a project deter you from volunteering for it. Don't let the fact that someone doesn't know you deter you from introducing yourself. Don't let the fact that something isn't the "usual process" deter you from trying it. When you join a company, you have the benefit of being that eager new hire who is still learning. Expectations of you will never be lower, so you might as well set expectations on your terms. Know the rules. Then bend them.

But a warning: Curiosity and entitlement are not the same thing. Asking for something genuinely without expecting it is always allowed. But expecting something—or demanding something or being overly disappointed if the answer is "no"—can be dangerous for your compatibility. If your reaction to "no" can be "No worries—just thought I'd ask" and not "How come?! That's ridiculous!" then give it a shot. As the saying goes, we are each the hero of our own journey and everyone else is but a supporting character. People are too busy thinking about themselves to be thinking about you. Think like an owner. If you don't look after your career, no one else will.

Context matters as well. If you are a woman in a male-dominated work setting, you may not get credited for your hard work. If you are performing a job that doesn't fit with the racial, gender, or other stereotypes of you (like if you are an Asian in a more people-oriented and less technically oriented role), people may not assume you're competent. If you are one of several "supporting characters" who are also trying to get noticed, you may need to maneuver your way into the spotlight. And if you are among coworkers who know people higher up in the organization, you may be vying for a limited set of opportunities. For example, an early-career professional told me that on his first day at an investment firm, the CEO of the company approached one of interns and said, "Oh, are you John's son? Let's get lunch!" Many of the people who'd worked for years in the company hadn't gotten a chance like that. If you happen to be in such a position, congratulations! Take advantage of the opportunity. But what if you aren't?

A college president once told me, "Some people need to be *less* entitled. Some people need to be *more* entitled." When that investment intern returns from his lunch with the CEO, he might want to go out of his way not to act entitled—and try even harder to show that he wants to learn, help, and do what he is told. After all, he just got an opportunity that his own manager may not have had. If he asks for more, he might risk overshooting his Three Cs.

For others, it may be worthwhile to be more entitled: If you want it, strive for it. If you aren't sure you can have it, ask for it.

It comes down to showing commitment without compromising your compatibility. You want to communicate that you are ready to learn and help—that you are ready and eager for more. The more people see that you want to improve yourself, the more they will want to help you improve. The more you demonstrate that you want to rise above your circumstances, the more people will want to help you do it.

In short, it's all about having the mindset of "Let's give this a shot." Do you have a crazy idea that probably won't work—but might work? Let's give this a shot. Is there something you'll probably fail at—but might succeed at? Let's give this a shot. Is there something you probably won't like—but might like? Let's give this a shot.

Think back to the last time you seized an opportunity that led to something even better. Did you land your current job by talking to someone you don't usually talk to? Did you meet your significant other at an event you almost didn't go to? Or, like me and Sandy (who opened my eyes to the unspoken rules), did you learn something by asking a question you almost didn't ask? If so, you've already experienced the power of "Let's give this a shot." Now it's time to bring this same mindset to your new job—and to keep it with you for the rest of your career.

Try This

- **Tell yourself:** where you start off does not have to dictate where you end up.

- **Tell yourself:** if you want more than the bare minimum, you'll need to do more than the bare minimum.

- **Tell yourself:** if the worst thing that can happen is the other person says "no," the risk of failure is probably not as bad as you think.

Show Up Like a High Performer

S hortly after Sana, an operations manager at a ride-hailing startup, received her job offer from HR, the emails started arriving. First came her future manager. Then came others in the company. In total, five people emailed her, and they all told her the same thing: "Let me know if you have any questions!" *You're kidding, right?* Sana thought to herself. *I just sat through seven interviews. I've already asked questions!*

Then something occurred to her. *What if asking more questions wasn't a chore, but an opportunity to build relationships?* Sana opened her laptop and scheduled a call with each person.

Before each call, she searched for the person online, scrolled through their LinkedIn profile, and skimmed their blog posts. She then came up with a list of questions to ask. Sana turned those five emails into five conversations—and, in turn, five new allies. So her first day didn't feel like a first day at all. She already knew what the company was up to. She already knew people across multiple teams—people she could now go to with questions. She even got involved in a product launch campaign led by someone she had met over the phone.

Day one for Sana could not look more different from day one for George, an intern at a bank. George was in the elevator with a coworker when it stopped—and the CEO of the bank walked in. George had no

Know This

- It is possible to make a positive first impression even before your first day.

- Show up to your first day knowing what your organization does, what it's been up to lately, who its competitors are, who the most important people are, and how their roles fit into the big picture.

- Always have a question—and make sure it's a good one.

idea who the CEO was, so he kept staring at the floor number on the elevator display. The CEO noticed that George was still wearing his name tag from training and turned to greet him. "Hi, I don't think we've met," the CEO said. "I'm Kathy."

"Hi, I'm George."

"Nice to meet you, George. Welcome," the CEO replied. "Which team do you report to?"

"I'm in asset management," George replied. "What about you?"

Kathy chuckled. "Oh, I'm the CEO."

George's eyes widened. His face turned bright red.

Later, George's coworker joked about the incident with the team. Within hours, everyone in the department had heard the story. For the rest of the summer, George was known as "the intern who didn't know the CEO."

When I heard George's story, my immediate reaction was, *Wow, that's harsh! Are people really that judgmental?* The answer is both no and yes.

Let's start with no. No, blowing that first impression doesn't mean you're doomed and should look for another job. The CEO herself has probably messed up a first impression at some point in her career. More important is how you respond. Do you shrivel up like a wilting flower? Or, do you poke fun at yourself with a line like, "Wow, I guess I'm *that* intern! I guess I need to do my homework! On the bright side, I hope this means I'm memorable?" One reaction makes people question your confidence. Another hints that you are self-aware enough to own up to your mistake—and mature enough to move on.

Now for the yes. As George's experience showed, yes, people judge. And they often do so without even realizing it.

Sana looked like a professional. George looked like a stereotypical intern—a kid in a suit. Sana flexed her Three Cs. George missed the opportunity. How can you be more like Sana and less like George? Think one step ahead—and see the big picture. I've come up with fifteen strategies to help you. Don't worry—most of them are quick. I suggest turning the first ten into habits whenever you are preparing for a new role, a networking call, a professional meeting, or a job interview. For email templates and talking points, visit gorick.com.

HIGHER-PRIORITY TASKS. Total time: forty-five minutes.

☐ Skim the Wikipedia page of the organization where the person you will be talking to works. This will help you understand the organization's work and history.

☐ Go to the organization's website and skim the "About us," "What we do," and "News" pages. This will help you understand how the organization describes itself.

☐ Search for the organization on http://www.google.com/news and skim any articles from the last few months. This will help you understand what the organization has been up to lately.

☐ Skim the titles, faces, and biographies of people listed on the "Team" page of the organization's website. Remember the names and faces of at least the head of the organization, the head of your department, and the head of your team. This will help you identify the most important people if you ever encounter them.

☐ Search for any emails you've received from the organization and note any individuals who were mentioned or CC'd. Then search online for each person's name + the organization + "LinkedIn" (e.g., John Smith [Organization Name] LinkedIn). This will help you identify possible conversation topics with your future coworkers.

☐ Observe how employees of the organization dress in images on the organization's social media accounts and videos on YouTube. Check with your HR contact that what you plan to wear is appropriate. (If you are working remotely, you probably only need to worry about this above the waist.) This will help you look like an insider.

☐ If you are showing up in person, reread your emails to make sure you are clear on where you need to go, when you need to arrive, and what you need to bring on your first day (photo ID, work visa, etc.). Then, look up the workplace address and figure out when to leave so that you arrive at least fifteen minutes early. This will help you avoid scrambling (or, worse, being late).

☐ Go to https://www.google.com/alerts and create a Google Alert for your organization. This will help you stay on top of the latest news.

☐ If your organization has a blog or email newsletter, subscribe to it. This will help you stay on top of what is happening at the organization.

☐ If anyone contacts you to offer to chat, accept their offer. This will help you build relationships early, not to mention better understand what to expect. (This will take some time, but don't squander the opportunity!)

LOWER-PRIORITY TASKS. These could take a few hours depending on your availability and level of ambition.

☐ Search online for your organization + "competitors" to find out who its rivals are. Browse their websites and try to understand how they are different. Consider going to https://www.google.com/alerts and setting up a Google Alert for each competitor as well. This will help you understand how your organization fits into the bigger picture.

☐ If you come across anyone at your organization who has a lot in common with you and with whom you have a mutual connection on LinkedIn, ask your connection to introduce you. This will help you find mentors and allies you can relate to.

☐ If you don't have a mutual connection with someone you want to talk to, try guessing their email address and cold emailing them to ask for a thirty-minute call to talk about their job and experiences.

☐ At the end of every call, ask, "Is there anyone else you'd suggest I speak with?" Then, ask if they can introduce you.

☐ Search for your organization on Glassdoor (to read employees' reviews), Reddit (to learn about public perception of the organization), and your favorite podcast app (to hear leaders from your organization speak about the organization's work).

The idea behind this exercise isn't to unearth every last detail about your team. It's simply to gather enough information that you can fill in the eight blanks in figure 3-1, which force you to take a step back and see the big picture. This is what the higher-ups in your organization do every day. The sooner you can adopt this mindset, the stronger the signal you send that you are competent and committed—and the more people will see you as a thought partner and not just a workhorse.

How to Ask Good Questions

Of course, it's not enough to do all this background research and tuck the knowledge away in your head. People can't read your mind, so they can't give you credit for your hard work unless you share what you know. This doesn't mean going around telling people how to do their jobs like some overbearing newbie, though, because that would be, well, overbearing.

It means asking questions. It's an unspoken rule: "Do you have any questions?" is not a "yes" or "no" question. It is a "yes" question. You should always have a question. But it's not just about asking questions. It's about asking *good* questions.

Knowing the difference between good and bad questions is critical. As much as people like to say "there are no stupid questions," there are. Here's how a product operations manager at a technology company described it

FIGURE 3-1

Blanks to fill in to see the big picture

- _____ helps _____ to _____ by _____ .
  My employer/client   these people   do these things   these methods

    E.g., ABC Ad Agency helps nonprofits increase donations by designing social media campaigns.

- Recently, _____ has been _____ to _____ .
            my employer/client   pursuing these initiatives   accomplish these goals

    E.g., Recently, ABC Ad Agency has been expanding to Asia to become a global name.

- _____ competes with _____ because _____ .
  My employer/client   these competitors   of these reasons

    E.g., ABC Ad Agency competes with XYZ Corp. because they both focus on awareness campaigns.

- _____ leads the company. _____ leads my department.
  This person   This person

    _____ leads my team.
  This person

    E.g., Ken R. (CEO) leads the company. Jerren C. (SVP, Marketing) leads the department. Angel A. leads my team.

- _____ is similar to me because _____ .
  This person   of these reasons

    E.g., Nisha, the designer on my team, is similar to me because we both grew up in Toronto.

- In my research, I learned _____ , which makes me curious about _____ ,
                           this thing   these things

    because _____ .
          of these reasons

    E.g., In my research, I learned that ABC just launched a podcast, which makes me curious about whether the team needs production help, because I used to work with my school's radio station.

- As a(n) _____ , I help _____ .
         this position   the team/department/company accomplish these goals

    E.g., As an executive assistant, I help senior leaders stay organized and get things done.

- On my first day, I will bring _____ , wear _____ , and show up at
                               these things   these clothes

    _____ at _____ .
  this place   this time

    E.g., On my first day, I will bring my ID, wear business casual, and show up at 26 Plympton St. at 8:30 a.m.

FIGURE 3-2

How to distinguish between good questions and bad questions

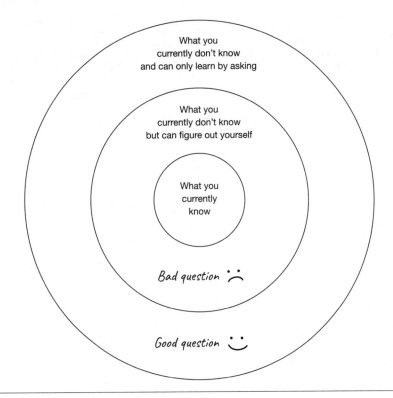

to me: "A stupid question is one where the answer is obvious, imminent, or easy to obtain. *Obvious* as in the answer has already been provided. *Imminent* as in questions like 'Are we there yet?' or 'Is it going to rain today?'—they will get answered within a short amount of time. *Easy to obtain* as in you can use a search engine or other resources to find the answer."

Picture a small circle, as in figure 3-2. The space inside the circle represents what you currently know. Now, picture a larger circle surrounding the smaller circle. This larger circle represents what you don't currently know but can figure out yourself. Any question that sits within this circle is a bad question, as the product operations manager I interviewed warned. These are the questions that make people think, *Oh, come on . . . I found the answer in ten seconds online (or by digging through my emails,*

FIGURE 3-3

How to explain where your questions come from

Which projects do you consider top priority? Which do you consider secondary priority?	+	I'm wondering because you said earlier that I'll be working with multiple people who might have their own priorities.
Here's my question.		*Here's why I'm asking this question.*

I saw in the public events calendar that we are hosting a conference next week.	+	Is there anything I can do to be helpful?
Here's what I know.		*Here's what I don't know.*

which you were CC'd on). If you can't figure this out yourself, what else will I need to do for you?

Finally, picture a third circle surrounding the other two. This circle represents what you don't know and can't learn by yourself, and therefore can only learn by asking. Any question you ask that sits within this circle but outside of the previous one is a good question. These are the questions that make people think, *I can see why you're wondering that. The answer can't be found anywhere a newbie like you would know about.*

Perception matters here too, of course. How "good" your question is depends on how well you can convince your listener that you couldn't have answered it on your own. The trick is the unspoken rule of *do—and show—your homework*: explain where your question is coming from before asking the question itself. So, instead of just asking your question, try going with the structure of "Here's my question, and here's why I'm asking this question." Or, "Here's what I know, and here's what I don't know," as seen in figure 3-3.

Sure, there's nothing stopping you from jumping straight into your question. But in doing so, you forgo the opportunity to subtly hint, *Hey, look how much work I've done to figure out what's going on!* Remember: people can't read your mind. It's like in school—you need to show your work to get partial credit. If you've taken the time to fill in the blanks from earlier in this chapter, you might as well cash in that hard work for some well-earned competence and commitment points. There's also an added bonus, according to the chief of staff at a financial technology startup: The more you ask good questions early, the more leeway you get to ask bad questions later.

If the list of instructions in this chapter makes you feel nervous or overwhelmed, keep in mind that the goal isn't just to follow some instructions. It's to build a set of habits—habits that may take time to form but that can serve you well for your entire career. Searching online to learn about an organization or individual can be time-consuming at first. Being on top of the latest news can be daunting at first. Asking questions—and showing off what you know—can feel scary at first. But, like all habits, they will become second nature before long. In my own career, I don't think twice before searching for recent news about a company or looking them up online. Start building these habits now!

Try This

- Before your first day at a job, skim the organization's website, especially the "About us," "What we do," "News," and "Team" pages, and search for the organization online and on social media. This will help you understand what your organization does, what it has been up to lately, and who the most important people are.

- Make sure you are clear on what you should wear, where you should go, when you should show up, and what you should bring for your first day.

- When you're new, focus on asking questions—specifically questions you can't answer yourself. Use the structure, "Here's my question, and here's why I'm asking this question" or "Here's what I know, and here's what I don't know."

Be Proactive

Starting a new role or project can feel like a first day of school (where introductions take place and you are given the instructions you need), a first day in a foreign country (where no one knows who you are), or a combination of the two. No matter what situation you find yourself in, however, the lesson is the same: No one will care more about your success than you—and no one will know more about what you need than you. You can't just sit around and wait for opportunities to come to you. You need to think like an owner.

Learn Your Job

On his first day in a rotational trainee program at a brewing company, Jabril picked up his name tag, backpack, laptop, branded water bottle, and training schedule. As soon as he logged into his computer, Jabril found a welcome message from his manager, along with a mass email introducing him and his fellow trainees to the entire company.

On her first day at an oil field, Valeria was greeted by a question she wasn't expecting: "Who are you?" It turned out that the site supervisor either hadn't been told of her arrival or forgot.

Jabril experienced the "first day of school" flavor of starting a job. Valeria, on the other hand, experienced the "first day in a new country" version. Chances are, your first day will fall somewhere between those two.

Know This

- Some managers are more thorough than others at getting you set up in a new project or role.

- If you aren't told what you need to do, go figure things out on your own.

- Showing that you want to help and learn can be an effective way to convince your teammates of your commitment.

Whether you are guided by a coworker or are left to figure out everything on your own, your goal is to be able to say "Yes!" to twelve questions. It might take some time, but with the guidance below you will be well on your way. Let's discuss what these questions are and what you can do to answer them if no one helps you.

Have I submitted my paperwork?

Whether it's signing up for retirement plans, setting up your direct deposit, or making sure your work visa paperwork is handled properly, be sure you have the basics done. If you aren't sure of something, ask HR or a coworker at your level. If there is one thing big companies are good at, it is paperwork—so expect lots of it. If you work at a startup, however, expect more chaos. In these cases, you can't always expect people to organize everything for you. You may have to get organized yourself.

Have I met my supervisor(s)?

If you don't know who your supervisor is, ask around with a question like, "Who will I be reporting to?" Once you meet them, try asking, "Is there anyone else I'll be expected to report to on a day-to-day basis?" If you aren't offered a meeting with your manager(s), try asking, "Would you have thirty to sixty minutes in the next few days to chat? I'd love to get to know you better and learn about expectations for my role."

Have I clarified my reporting lines?

If you have multiple supervisors and will be juggling projects for them simultaneously, it's a good idea to ask, "How would you suggest I allocate my time between you and [my other manager]? Fifty-fifty? Sixty-forty?" And if you have a desk job, ask, "What's the best way to keep you all in the loop? Would it be helpful for me to CC you on emails or share regular updates?" These questions can help you prevent each supervisor from assuming that you are 100 percent devoted to them—and potentially overworking you.

Have I clarified expectations for my role?

If you are filling a new role (e.g., you are the first recruiter the team has hired), then you will want to understand why your position was created, what your mandate is (how you are expected to do more, better, faster, or cheaper), and how things have typically been done in the past.

If you are filling an existing role, then you will want to understand what your predecessor did and how they did it. That way you can do the job just as well—or better. If you are filling a project-based role with a defined end date (e.g., you are an intern, a consultant, a temp, or a contractor), then you will want to know what you are expected to contribute and with what frequency and quality. Here are five questions to consider asking:

- "Which tasks and deliverables are top priorities in my role? Which ones are secondary?"

- "What should I be able to do by the end of the first three months? Six months?"

- "What does success look like in my role? Are there any metrics I should keep in mind?"

- "Is there anyone else you'd suggest I introduce myself to?"

- "What should day-to-day and week-to-week collaboration look like between us? When should I be proactive and when should I be reactive?"

Have I found a regular interaction schedule with my manager?

If your manager doesn't mention one-on-one meetings, consider asking, "Would it be helpful for us to have some sort of regular check-in?" followed by "What's most convenient: weekly, biweekly, monthly?" If your manager doesn't see the value of one-on-ones, then you may need to find excuses to interact more informally, whether over coffee, after meetings, or casually during the workday.

If you are working as a temp or a contractor on a specific project, consider asking your manager, "Would it be helpful to schedule a midway check-in?" And if you're hoping to transition to a full-time job, it's important to let your manager know that you are committed to staying long term.

Have I introduced myself to my coworkers?

If you are working in person, consider walking around and saying, "Hi, I don't think we've met. I'm _____. I'm the new _____" to those near you, on your team, and on any other teams you work with.

If you are working remotely, consider sending your teammates a short email or instant message (depending on your team's cultural norms) introducing yourself. If you are taking over for someone, consider asking your manager to introduce you, assuming they are still in the organization and are eager to help. If there is a receptionist or a security guard on-site, consider introducing yourself to them, too. They are important people to know if you ever get locked out or need help navigating the system.

Have I learned my team's priorities?

As you meet your teammates, consider asking, "What are you currently working on?" or "What are your and the team's top priorities these days?" The better you understand what everyone is working on and stressed out about, the better you will be at finding ways to make yourself useful.

Have I defined my day-to-day work schedule?

If you are working in person, consider asking coworkers at your level, "When do folks typically arrive and leave?" You can also try to recognize patterns around when people send emails. For example, does it happen only during business hours? (This strategy helps if you're working remotely, too.)

Have I set up my workspace, tools, and access?

Is there equipment you will need to do your job, such as an ID card or electronic devices, uniforms, safety gear, company vehicles, or tools? Is there software you will need to install, like instant messenger, email, video chat, file sharing, printer drivers, or project management software? Consider setting them all up now so you won't need to scramble later, when you actually need them. If your organization is large, there should be IT and HR departments to guide you. If your organization is small, then it may be up to you to figure it out.

Have I gotten access to the necessary files and calendar invitations?

If you are taking over for someone and haven't been given access to their files, consider asking your manager, "Did my predecessor leave behind any files that I should go through?" If your team uses a shared drive and no one has invited you, ask a coworker at your level, "Would you please be able to grant me access?," "Are there particular folders that I should familiarize myself with?," and "Are there any templates you all use that I should keep handy?" While you are at it, make sure to ask, "Are there any upcoming meetings I should be looped in on?"

Have I navigated my work environment?

If you are working in person and no one offers you a tour, consider walking around and making note of key managers' offices, relevant coworkers' workstations, meeting rooms, bathrooms, break rooms, stairwells, and elevators. This will help you stay near the action, strategically bump into people, and avoid getting lost on your way to a meeting. If you are working remotely, consider setting up a dedicated workspace where you can minimize distractions, keep good posture, get a good amount of (ideally natural) light, and have a professional backdrop for video calls.

Have I sorted out my daily routine?

If you are working in person, do you need to arrange transportation to and from work? Will you need to arrange for child care? Do you need a parking pass? If you are working from home, what will your exercise routine be? When will you prepare food? You may be able to answer these questions without the help of your manager or coworkers, but they are important to consider in your early days because they will affect your productivity and happiness.

While the ramping-up period of starting a new job can be structured, it can also be unstructured—and even chaotic. If you are given time to get settled, take it; if you aren't given time, return to this list whenever you have the chance. If you are given instructions, do as you are told. If you aren't given instructions, think like an owner and figure it out. It can feel awkward to bother your busy coworkers, but consider this: your success is in everyone's interest—and you can succeed only if you are set up for success. You aren't being annoying. You're demonstrating your commitment.

Find Your Job

So, you've figured out how to answer "yes" to the above questions. Now, it's time to start making yourself useful. Although every team will want you to be as productive as soon as possible, not all teams will know how to make it happen. Your teammates may reach out to you, but they may not have a plan for you. They may explain some things, but they may not explain everything. They may assign you tasks, but they may not give you responsibilities.

The problem of not knowing what to do is especially common if you are working from home. Unless your organization has a long history of people working remotely, chances are your supervisor is still trying to figure out how to properly manage remote employees. In such a case, you will need to figure out some things on your own—so don't let others' busyness prevent you from finding your role on the team. Let's walk through three strategies you can use to get started on your work.

Observe others and take notes

Pay attention to what your manager and teammates are up to, and if you don't already have an assignment, try asking, "Would it be helpful for me to join this meeting?" or "Mind if I observe how you do this?" Then take notes (by hand if others don't have their electronic devices out).

If you are working remotely, listen closely during team calls when others speak about upcoming meetings or projects. Consider emailing or messaging your teammates and saying, "I'd love to learn more about _____. Is there any room for me to be involved?" If you don't have team meetings to observe while working remotely, consider telling your manager, "I just finished setting up and would love to learn how things work on the team. Are there any meetings you'd suggest I join?"

Ask questions and learn from the answers

As you observe your coworkers and learn your job, keep a list of questions on topics you are curious or confused about. (See figure 4-1 for some examples.) Do—then show—your homework.

As a newcomer, it can be tempting to stay quiet out of fear of bothering people or looking clueless. Actually, staying quiet is the opposite of what people expect. At any point in a job you will be in one of two modes: learner and leader.

Learner mode is when people know that you don't know much yet, so they expect you to ask questions. Leader mode is when you've been around for long enough that people expect you to know what's going on and to ask thoughtful questions and make thoughtful comments. You are always in learner mode when you are new to a team or project, so people know you will have questions. Always have questions.

A friendly caution: While questions can be a simple, effective way to show your commitment, they aren't just for show. They are also for your learning. Take notes and remember what others tell you!

FIGURE 4-1

Questions to try asking when you are new

- *What did* _____ *mean by* _____ *?*
  this person   this term or statement

- *What is the history of* _____ *?*
          this decision

- *How does* _____ *work?*
     this process

- *How does what* _____ *said about* _____ *align with what* _____
         this person   this topic   that person
  said about _____ *?*
     that topic

- _____ *was an unfamiliar face/name. Who are they?*
  This person

Embrace and volunteer for work

Often, meetings lead to new work. And often your supervisor won't have time to do all of this work themselves. Sometimes they will delegate the work to you—and you'll be expected to do as you're told. Other times, you may need to ask to be involved. Either way, new projects are opportunities to prove your competence and show your commitment. If you are interested in something that was discussed in a meeting, consider approaching your manager after the meeting and asking any of the questions in figure 4-2.

If you aren't in any meetings where work is generated, then try paying attention when others complain—these may be hidden opportunities for you to make yourself useful. If you spot an opportunity, consider asking, "Can I help?" or "I noticed _____. Is there anything I can do to help?" or "How can I be helpful?"

Or, if it isn't possible to observe people because you are remote, consider emailing or messaging your manager and saying, "I just finished

FIGURE 4-2

Questions to try asking after meetings

- _____ mentioned that we should _____ . Should I follow up?
  This person   do this

- Would it make sense for me to _____ given the discussion about _____ ?
                                 do this   this topic

- _____ asked _____. Do we need to get back to them?
  This person   this question

- _____ expressed curiosity about _____. Should I look into it?
  This person   this topic

- As a next step, would it be helpful for me to follow up with _____
                                                              this person

  about _____ ?
        this topic

---

with _____ and would be happy to contribute in any way I can. Do you have any projects where you could use an extra pair of hands?"

But be careful: Volunteer only if you have time. You get credit for your commitment without sacrificing your competence only if you do what you say you will do. Another caution: while it may be up to you to volunteer for tasks, it often isn't up to you if a higher-up "voluntells" you for a task by assigning it, but making it look like it is optional for you to accept it. When you are new, "Can you do this?" isn't a "yes" or "no" question. It's a "Yes!" question. And ideally, your answer is "Yes! And would it be helpful if I also did _____?" When you are new, tedious tasks are more than tedious tasks; they are mini tests of your competence and commitment.

Starting a new role is stressful enough as it is. Managers who leave you to get set up yourself—what should be their responsibility—don't make life any easier. But herein lies a key difference between school and work: school is about *keeping up*; work is about *stepping up*. In school, you are rewarded for following instructions—simply show up to class, listen, read the textbook, and submit your homework by the deadline and you'll be a star. In the workplace, there is no syllabus, no textbook, no clearly numbered list of homework problems to complete. Sometimes, people are so busy meeting their own deadlines that they may not even notice that a new member of the team has shown up. And sometimes, despite their best intentions to set you up for success, even the best of managers can look forgetful and uncaring when their own managers summon them for that surprise meeting minutes before you arrive. The result? The workplace favors the proactive. If no one steps up to help you, step up and help yourself.

Try This

- If no one introduces themselves, you introduce yourself.

- If no one shares information with you, you ask for the information.

- If no one finds you work, you find the work.

SECRETS TO

SHAPING
OTHERS'
PERCEPTIONS

Know How to Tell Your Story

O n Meghan's first day as a co-op student at a biotechnology company, her manager asked, "So, what do you want to do here?"

Meghan froze. *What?!* she thought. *I figured you'd already have a project for me!* Not knowing how to respond, Meghan said, "Anything you want! I'm flexible." However, when she tried to update her résumé at the end of the six-month co-op, she found herself staring at the blinking cursor, unsure of what to write.

What did Meghan do during her co-op? She cleaned a bunch of spreadsheets, sent a bunch of emails, and summarized a bunch of research papers. It wasn't the résumé-building experience she had imagined. Looking back, Meghan told me: "Had I done more research into what the organization did and thought more about what I wanted, I would've been able to suggest my own ideas and maybe even get the experience I wanted. Instead, I made them think up what work to give me, which probably led to work I didn't want and results they didn't care about."

Interacting with your coworkers as a new team member can be like interacting with reporters as a celebrity. People will bombard you with questions and analyze your every response. It's important to take these questions seriously. Your responses could determine whether you get the

Know This

- The clearer you are on what you want from your new role, the better your chances of designing a fulfilling experience for yourself.

- The better you can explain how your past, present, and future selves fit with your job, the more competent and committed you will come across.

experience you want—or the experience others want. How can you avoid ending up in Meghan's situation? By learning how to tell your story.

Internal Narrative versus External Narrative

Before we continue, it's important to understand the difference between your *internal* narrative and your *external* narrative. Your internal narrative is the story you tell yourself about why you do the things you do. It's what convinced you to accept the job you did. It's also what nudges you to get out of bed in the morning and hustle at work. Your internal narrative could, for example, sound like, "I want to make money to pay off my student loans, get work experience, and figure out whether I like lab work." Or "I'm here because this was the only job I could get."

Your external narrative, on the other hand, is the story you tailor to your audience to convince others that you are competent, committed, and compatible. Your external narrative might sound like, "The company's work in Alzheimer's disease is especially interesting to me because neuroscience was one of my favorite classes in college. I also volunteered at an eldercare facility and saw the effects of Alzheimer's on my grandfather, so I have a personal connection to it."

Notice the difference. Your internal narrative translates into nothing more than "me," "me," "me." Your external narrative, on the other hand, translates into "This is what I want . . . and this is how I am competent in and committed to this work."

Why not just tell people your internal narrative? If all others hear is "I'm only here for me," then it can be easy for them to question your commitment and compatibility. And if they hear "I don't know" (as Meghan's manager did), then it can be easy for them to think, *Hmm . . . let me think about this*—only to forget to follow up. In fact, if you've ever been ghosted by a recruiter after a call or interview, it may be because you shared too much of your internal narrative and not enough of your external narrative. This is not to say that your internal and external narratives are separate and distinct, though. They can—and often will—overlap. The degree of overlap comes down to how closely your role resembles your dream job. If your role is a means to an end, you risk sounding selfish if you keep emphasizing your internal narrative. To avoid being seen as uncommitted or incompatible, consider focusing on your external narrative instead.

Table 5-1 lists a common set of questions you can expect to be asked when you are new to a role, team, or project. Each question means more than its literal meaning. In fact, behind each question is a hidden opportunity for you to show your Three Cs and, in turn, get what you want.

The questions may seem overwhelming at first, but answering them will eventually become second nature. The key isn't to memorize any answers. Instead, it's to know your personal story well enough that you have talking points ready no matter what questions others ask. To build these talking points, practice the following five steps.

Step 1: Build Your Internal Narrative

Work backward from the end goal: imagine how you'll look back at your work experience on your last day. What will you want to have done? Next, try to fill in the blanks in figure 5-1. Don't worry if you don't have everything figured out. Your internal narrative isn't static. It's meant to evolve over time as you learn more about yourself. More important is that you put something on paper that you can refer back to. If Meghan had asked herself what she really wanted from the co-op experience, she would have communicated better with her coworkers— and, in doing so, increased her odds of designing a fulfilling experience. It's like going shopping: you are more likely to walk out with what you want if you bring a list.

TABLE 5-1

Questions you can expect to be asked when you're new

	What you'd share if you interpreted the question literally	What you'd share if you tailored your message to your audience
Tell me about yourself. Or, what's your story?	Where you were born, where you were raised, and where you went to school	How your prior experiences led to you being competent in and committed to your new role
What brought you to our organization?	How you actually heard about the job	How your prior experiences led you to seek out this opportunity
What got you interested in this role?	What you want to gain from this experience	How you are drawn to the work and mission of the team and organization
What kind of work are you interested in? Or, what do you want to do here?	What type of work you are and are not interested in	What specific areas of the team's or organization's work you are interested in and how you'll be able to contribute based on your strengths and interests
What are you hoping to get out of this experience?	What your honest reasons are for taking this job	How you are interested in learning and helping
What prior experience do you have?	Where you've worked (or "none")	How whatever you've done has led to you being interested in this role and how the knowledge and skills you've acquired translate to your new role
Where do you see yourself in the future?	How you are using the job as a stepping-stone	How you plan to progress at the firm and take on additional responsibilities

Step 2: Build Your External Narrative

Once you have your internal narrative, the next step is to turn it into a set of talking points that you can tailor to your audience for your external narrative. Use what you just learned about yourself to fill in the blanks in figure 5-2. Remember: you want to show your competence and commitment. Fill in the blanks with details that are relevant to your job. In a data-crunching role, talk about your experience or interest in data and analysis. If you don't have much (or any) experience, that's OK—focus on telling people what you want to learn. Resist the urge to remind people

FIGURE 5-1

Blanks to fill in to build your internal narrative

- *I'm in this job because* _____.
  of these reasons

  E.g., I'm in this job because I want the work experience and it pays well.

- *I want to test* _____.
  these hypotheses

  E.g., I want to test whether I'd enjoy working in biotech research.

- *I want to meet* _____.
  these types of people

  E.g., I want to meet a mentor and maybe someone who can write my grad school reference letter.

- *I want to develop* _____.
  these types of skills

  E.g., I want to develop my laboratory research skills.

- *I want to learn about* _____.
  these types of topics

  E.g., I want to learn about how a lab works and how science gets commercialized.

- *I want to be able to say that I* _____ *on my résumé.*
  did these things

  E.g., I want to be able to say that I helped design and run a laboratory experiment on my résumé.

---

of any shortcomings: talking about how you've never handled numbers before makes it easy for people to question your competence. No one has to know. Focus on the positive.

An effective way to show your competence and commitment is to highlight commonalities between what you've done in the past and what you're about to do in your new role. The key is to emphasize your transferable skills—you do have them, no matter what your work experience is. Been a babysitter? Talk about what responsibility means to you. Been a tutor? Talk about the art of putting complicated concepts in simple terms. Been a cashier, retail sales associate, barista, or server? Talk about what it takes to work with people and multitask under pressure.

FIGURE 5-2

Blanks to fill in to build your external narrative

- My name is ___ and I'm a _____ on ___, which means that I _____.

           name   *position*   *team*   *do these things*

    E.g., My name is Tiana and I'm a research co-op on the DNA sequencing team, which means that I help the team conduct experiments and publish their research.

- I became interested in this opportunity after _____.

                                         this experience/observation

    E.g., I became interested in this opportunity after taking a college class on bioinformatics and reading about this lab's work in the news.

- Before this, I was at _____, where I _____.

                         prior experience   *did these relevant things*

    E.g., Before this, I was at a research lab at my college, where I helped a professor on her *Nature* journal article.

- Your work in _____ is especially interesting to me because _____.

                 this area   *of these reasons*

    E.g., Your work in cancer therapeutics is especially interesting to me because I'm exploring a career in this area and your lab is on the cutting edge of interventions.

- I'm curious about _____ and would love exposure to _____.

                       these topics   *this type of work*

    E.g., I'm curious about how research gets published and would love exposure to how you turn lab research into publishable articles.

- If you come across opportunities to _____ or _____, I'd love for you to keep

                                           do this   *do that*

me in mind.

    E.g., If you come across opportunities to help design experiments or write articles, I'd love for you to keep me in mind.

In the future

- I'd love to _____.

              do this/become this

    E.g., I'd love to become a professor.

- I'm still exploring, but so far _____ and _____ seem interesting to me.

                                   this area   *that area*

    E.g., I'm still exploring, but so far academia and the pharmaceutical industry seem interesting to me.

Once you've finished building your internal and external narratives, you will have all the raw ingredients necessary to answer any questions others may ask when you are new. I think of my brainstorming as a "refrigerator" of different talking points. Any time someone asks me a question, all I have to do is open my mental fridge and pull out the "ingredient" (talking point) that best fits the situation.

If you like your fridge organized, try this: take all the ingredients in your fridge and relate them back to why you are competent, committed, and compatible. Try it out by filling in the following three sentences.

Competence: "I have what it takes to succeed here because _____."

Commitment: "I am excited to be here because _____."

Compatibility: "I belong in this role and team because _____."

Step 3: Add Structure

What if others ask a forward-looking question like "What kind of work are you interested in?" Do your homework, then show your homework. And don't just use ingredients from your fridge—include details from the online research you did in chapter 3. It may seem like a small difference, but going from "I'd love exposure to clinical trials" to "I'd love exposure to clinical trials; if I'm not mistaken, I believe one of your drugs just entered this process?" can be all it takes to go from merely answering the question to both answering the question and underscoring your commitment.

If others ask a backward-looking question like "What brought you to our company?" then consider framing your story using the structure of past, present, future. This past, present, future arc to storytelling is inspired by what's called the Hero's Journey or Heroine's Journey, which is the backbone of many famous tales: Frodo Baggins in *The Lord of the Rings* leaves the Shire to destroy the One Ring; Anna in *Frozen* leaves Arendelle to find her sister Elsa and to bring back summer; Harry Potter trains at Hogwarts to defeat Voldemort. Take a snapshot of any of

FIGURE 5-3

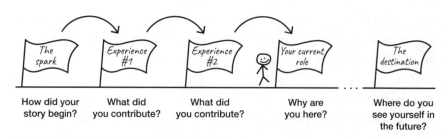

How to tell your Hero's Journey

The spark	Experience #1	Experience #2	Your current role	The destination
How did your story begin?	What did you contribute?	What did you contribute?	Why are you here?	Where do you see yourself in the future?

these stories and you'll see the same elements: where the hero comes from (their past), what they are up to now (their present), and what goal they are trying to achieve (their future). What "quest" are you on? That's your Hero's Journey. Figure 5-3 offers a framework for thinking about the elements of your quest.

I often get questions about where the start of your Hero's Journey should be. There is no set rule, so find the most relevant point. Maybe your interest in startups began with the dog-walking business you had as a kid. OK, start there—but skip forward quickly so your story takes two minutes to tell—not twenty. But maybe your interest didn't begin until a certain class, internship, or news article you read. That's OK too. Feel out the culture of your team to assess how personal people are with their stories. Some cultures will appreciate journeys that bring up personal details like family. Others will want stories that are strictly professional.

Step 4: Finesse Your Style

Now that we have the storytelling substance and structure down, let's talk about style. The key is to avoid overshooting or undershooting your zones of competence, commitment, and compatibility whenever you talk about yourself.

FIGURE 5-4

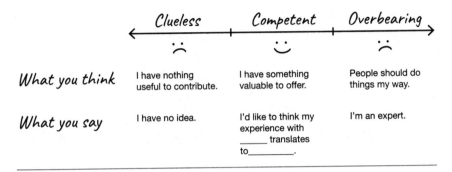

How to maintain your competence when talking about yourself

	Clueless	Competent	Overbearing
What you think	I have nothing useful to contribute.	I have something valuable to offer.	People should do things my way.
What you say	I have no idea.	I'd like to think my experience with _____ translates to _____.	I'm an expert.

Maintaining your competence

Make it clear that you have something to offer and are doing important work—without coming across as if you either know what's best or have no idea what's going on. This means saying "I'd like to think my experience with _____ translates to _____" or "I will be working on _____" and not "I'm an expert at this" or "I have no clue." Figure 5-4 shows how what you say can make you come across as clueless, competent, or overbearing.

It's easy to overshoot or undershoot unintentionally. One time, a new manager at a startup kept starting his remarks with "Well, in my last job, I . . ." By the third instance, his coworkers had started a group text to complain about how stuck-up he was. This manager looked overbearing, not realizing that his coworkers were thinking, *If your last job was so great, why are you here?*

Another time, an intern in the US government was working beside her manager on an urgent matter when the office head entered the room.

"What's up?" the office head asked.

"Oh, not much!" the intern replied.

"What do you mean 'not much'?" the manager snapped. "We're dealing with a crisis!" This intern looked clueless, forgetting that, in the moment, "What's up?" actually meant "What are you working on?" and not the rhetorical "What's up?" that you might ask your friends.

Maintaining your commitment

Demonstrate that you are eager to learn, help, and grow without coming across as power-hungry, trying to take anyone's job, or looking to make anyone look bad. This means saying "I'm exploring a potential career in this area" or "I am curious about _____" and not "I will become CEO" or "I expect to get promoted." Figure 5-5 shows how what you say can make you come across as apathetic, committed, or threatening.

Again, it's easy to overshoot or undershoot. One time, a temp social worker at a community health center was asked by her manager, "What are your career plans?"

"I want to become the coordinator," this social worker replied.

Her manager frowned. "Uh . . . OK . . ."

This social worker had overlooked a critical detail: there was only one coordinator job at the facility—and her manager already held it with no plans to leave. The manager's "OK" didn't actually mean "OK." It meant, *So you're saying you want my job? How are you going to do that? By getting me fired?!* Luckily, many managers appreciate ambition and aren't this insecure. But you never know. If you aren't careful, it can be easy to look threatening.

Another time, a junior analyst at an economic research firm sat down with a senior analyst to discuss his first assignment. The senior analyst began to explain the process of cleaning and merging datasets. After

FIGURE 5-5

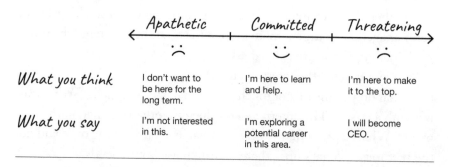

How to maintain your commitment when talking about yourself

	Apathetic	Committed	Threatening
What you think	I don't want to be here for the long term.	I'm here to learn and help.	I'm here to make it to the top.
What you say	I'm not interested in this.	I'm exploring a potential career in this area.	I will become CEO.

seeing the junior analyst sit there quietly without taking notes, the senior analyst asked, "Any questions?"

"Oh," the junior analyst replied. "I actually don't want to do these types of projects, so I don't think it's a good use of your time to teach me."

The junior analyst instantly seemed apathetic. This is what the senior analyst told me: "Just because a project doesn't align with your goals doesn't mean you can say no. We're a small firm. You can't behave like something's not your problem. Everything is everyone's problem."

Maintaining your compatibility

Make it clear that you are excited to be a member of the team without sounding like you are trying to do everything or be someone you aren't. This means saying "I'm excited to join the team!" or "Looking forward to getting to know you all!" and not "I love everything you just said!" or "Yes, I can do that! And that! And that too!" Figure 5-6 shows how what you say can make you come across as passive, compatible, or a poser.

Overshooting often involves being overeager to the point of sounding fake. For example, a quality assurance associate became known as a suck-up after people noticed he was overly enthusiastic—but only when a higher-up introduced anything. Whereas others offered the occasional nod or *mhmm*, this associate nodded excessively and said *mhmm* after almost every sentence. The first time, people found it odd. The second

FIGURE 5-6

How to maintain your compatibility when talking about yourself

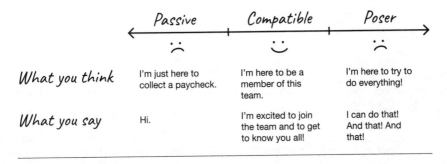

time, people found it annoying. The third time, people labeled him a poser.

Undershooting often involves not smiling enough or not sharing enough when you introduce yourself. At a staff meeting at a research lab, the new research assistants took turns introducing themselves. Everyone took at least a minute and talked enthusiastically about their favorite courses and research topics. However, one person simply said, "Hi, I'm Ethan," followed by a long pause. Ethan ended up being liked for his competence, but he had no idea that his colleagues kept wondering if he was shy, if he didn't like them, or if he was antisocial—because he seemed so passive. These judgments may not be fair, but they are real.

Nailing the Three Cs takes time. You'll need to practice, recognize patterns, and practice some more. Don't worry if you feel like you overshot or undershot at first. Observe the body language of your listeners. Pay attention to moments when people are frowning, crossing their arms, leaning back, shifting their gaze, or tilting their heads. These could be subtle hints for you to reframe your story next time. Look for smiles and nods too, since they mean your story is being received well. Then, use people's responses to further tweak your story. If you are doing your introduction over the phone and don't have the chance to observe others' expressions, try speaking slowly and pausing occasionally so that they can offer an *mhmm* or ask a question. By the time you get to your dozenth intro, you will be a pro.

Step 5: Practice!

Though *what* you say is important, *how* you say it can be just as crucial. This book isn't a public speaking guide, so we won't go into too much detail, but the key is to sound confident but not arrogant, proper but not robotic, and upbeat but not immature.[1]

Sound confident...

Sounding confident means sounding like you believe in what you have to say (which you will if you know the substance of your story). This also means looking people in the eye, gesturing smoothly, speaking at a calm pace, saying every word clearly, talking loudly enough that people can hear you, and avoiding "uptalking" (that is, not ending statements as if you are asking a question and instead ending with a downward intonation). In the words of an intern at a media company, "It's normal to be nervous. Act like you belong and people will start to believe it."

But not arrogant

Sounding arrogant means sounding like you think that you are better than other people. So, don't interrupt others—wait until others finish speaking to make your point. Be careful about rolling your eyes or sticking your chin up, and stand or sit so you're looking at people at eye level. Be mindful of your use of the condescending-sounding "Well . . ." or shooting down whatever others say with a "Yeah, but . . ."

Sound proper . . .

Sounding proper means sounding as mature and formal as your coworkers. Since maturity and formality can sound different depending on whether you're at a bank or a tech startup, follow your coworkers' lead. So, if others don't say "like," "you know," "you guys," "sweet," "awesome," "totally," "dude," "sup," "yup," "my bad," "chill," or ". . . right?" try to avoid these words too. If others don't use slang, avoid slang. If others don't swear, avoid swearing. If you aren't sure what it means to be formal in your workplace, play it safe and be more formal at first, then tone it down later. It's easier to shake off the perception that you're too serious than the perception that you're unprofessional.

But not robotic

Sounding robotic means sounding like you memorized a speech. So, while you should know what external narrative to pull from your fridge, you don't need to recite the back of the orange juice carton on command. If you can't remember something, move on—avoid freezing as if you forgot your line in a play. Be especially careful of clichés like "synergy," "innovative," and "disrupt" and vague statements that can apply to anything, like "I'm passionate about this company and its values" (unless you elaborate).

Sound upbeat...

Sounding upbeat means sounding energetic. This means letting your voice rise and fall (and not being monotone), speaking positively or at least neutrally about others (and not criticizing them), and keeping an open and engaging face (and not keeping a poker face).

But not immature

Sounding immature means sounding childish. This means observing patterns among your coworkers when it comes to their vocal pitch, level of excitement, and amount of giggling or laughing.

Practice helps in all of these areas, so try standing in front of the mirror, looking yourself in the eye, and rehearsing what you want to say. Or, practice with a friend. The key is to treat this section not as a set of rigid rules, but rather as a loose mental checklist for assessing yourself. But beware: like many of the hidden expectations that we discuss in this book, few will be fair. Is it about professionalism or is it about conformity? And to what extent is "professionalism" a matter of what we do versus a matter of who we are (in the case of people with naturally high-pitched voices, for example)? Double standards are also everywhere. When is your self-introduction about telling a compelling external narrative and when is it about suppressing your own true self? Clearly it's not just about telling your story. Until the day your manager embraces you for who you are—and not who they want you to be—know your audience and be deliberate about how you tell your story.

Although we're focused on answering common questions from your first days in a new role, the skills of knowing your audience and telling your story can serve you well in your entire career. You may not work in sales, but you're "selling" yourself every time you interact with someone. Start polishing your story now. Doing so not only can help you in your new job—it can help you land your next opportunity, role, or project.

Try This

- Write down your internal narrative: What do you want out of this experience?

- Be ready to share your external narrative: How does who you are and what you've done make you competent, committed, and compatible for your new role?

- Figure out what your audience is interested in hearing, then give them what they want.

- Frame your story in terms of past, present, future—just like a Hero's Journey.

- When speaking, try to be confident but not arrogant, proper but not robotic, and upbeat but not immature.

Manage Your Appearance

When I first arrived at my Wall Street internship, I didn't think much about how I looked. All I heard was that the dress code was "business formal," which I interpreted as any suit, any tie, any dress shirt, any leather belt, any socks, and any dress shoes.

Reality hit when I overheard my coworkers joking about how ill-fitting dress shirts, square-toed dress shoes, and belts that didn't match the color of one's shoes had no place on Wall Street. I looked down. They were describing my outfit.

Luckily, the workplace is becoming more casual and tolerant, especially with the shift to remote work. Still, the lesson remains: when it comes to your physical appearance at work, dress codes like "business casual" or "smart casual" tell only part of the story. It's the hidden expectations that can separate outsiders from insiders—and this goes far beyond clothes, to your hair, accessories, and even grooming choices. Since others' judgments can be unforgiving and enduring, it never hurts to be deliberate. After all, defining your identity should be your job—not others' job.

What can you do? It begins with figuring out what is appropriate to your workplace and what feels authentic to you.

Know This

Looking professional is all about finding the intersection of what's appropriate to your workplace and what feels authentic to you.

How to Figure Out What's Appropriate

The first step is to recognize patterns. Try to recall how others came across during your interview, and search for any company photos posted online. Identify common appearance choices across many, most, or all of the coworkers at your level. If you notice everyone wearing dresses or collared shirts, you may have spotted an unspoken dress code. If you notice a lack of cologne or perfume, you may have picked up on an unspoken norm about scent. If you notice there isn't a single wrinkle in others' clothes, you may have spotted something about tidiness.

And then mirror others. Use the patterns you identify to inform your wardrobe and grooming choices. Focus on important stylistic elements like clothing type, color, pattern, materials, fit, and tidiness over details like brand or price. Consider getting one outfit first, then expanding once you've learned the unspoken norms. If you are working remotely, focus on what will be visible during a video call.

When in doubt, ask a mentor or coworker, "Would _____ be appropriate?" If you are still in doubt when picking between two looks, consider starting with the more formal option. It's better to look too serious than unprofessional. (And you can always adjust your wardrobe down later.)

If you're still stuck, try putting yourself in your managers', coworkers', clients', and partners' shoes. Then look at yourself and ask, If I created a fashion catalog for my profession, would I include my look? The goal is to leave the insiders thinking, *Yes, I can take you seriously.* This means appearing appropriate—and not like you're trying too hard or not hard enough.

This is all easier said than done, of course. In general, jobs in the service sector or skilled trades will have more explicit rules like "black pants and shoes only," "must wear steel-toed boots," or "must cover your tattoos."

TABLE 6-1

What to consider when deciding your appearance

Clothes	• Tops, bottoms, headscarves, legwear, socks, shoes, outerwear
	• Color palette, patterns
	• Materials
	• Fit
	• Brands
	• Quality, cleanliness, newness, ironed (or not), tucked in (or not)
Accessories	• Jewelry, bags, belts, watches, scarves, shawls
Skin	• Makeup, tattoos, piercings
Grooming	• Hair, facial hair, nails, scent

If this is your situation, what counts as appropriate may be relatively easy to figure out. If you are in the white-collar world (where people typically work at a desk), however, brace yourself for unspoken expectations beyond the typical "don't wear a suit to that startup job" or "wear business casual or business formal to a finance job." Table 6-1 lists some of the elements of your appearance that are worth thinking about carefully.

These unspoken expectations can get quite nuanced and context-dependent. An outdoor education teacher told me, "People in the outdoors will judge both the brand and technical functionality of your gear. If you show up with an expensive jacket, but it's too puffy for the fall or not puffy enough for the winter, people will think you're a poser."

How to Determine What's Authentic to You

Although your colleagues' appearances can be a helpful starting point, they are merely that: an average and a starting point. Averages tell you how things have always been done—not how they could (or should) be. They tell you what's common among the majority—not what's authentic to you. They tell you what *others* do—not what *you* should do. This is important to keep in mind, especially if you don't share the same background as your coworkers. If you find yourself in a situation where your

FIGURE 6-1

Your options for deciding your appearance

	Reject the rules	Bend the rules	Embrace the rules
What you think	I am who I am. Take it or leave it.	I will meet you partway.	I will become a chameleon.
What you do	I will ignore others' appearances. If my team can't embrace me for who I am, this place isn't for me.	I will mirror my team as long as I do not compromise my identity/values, then perhaps reveal more of my identity as I establish myself.	I will mirror my team even if it means compromising my identity/values.

Decide where you want to be.

appearance doesn't "fit," what do you do: reject the rules, embrace the rules, or bend the rules? Figure 6-1 shows your options for navigating this question.

There are no right or wrong answers here—only personal values. There are plenty of people who've rejected, embraced, or bent the rules. Each of them has had to wrestle with their own obstacles and sacrifices.

Avery, a professional in the insurance industry, rejected the rules. They were assigned a male gender at birth, but identified as gender nonbinary. Whenever Avery had an interview, they showed up with long hair, earrings, and painted nails. Avery knew it would be difficult to present themselves as feminine within a body that was perceived to be male, so they wanted there to be no surprises around how they would dress if they got the job. And when a company didn't hire them, Avery took it as a sign that they wouldn't be happy there anyway. Once they did get a job offer, Avery spoke to HR and their manager before their first day to explain how important it was for them to be themselves. In Avery's words, "I established myself as a person who will not conform." But Avery's choice hasn't been without its sacrifices: "I've gotten along with my coworkers because I've proven my competence, but still—no one's willing to put me in a client-facing role out of a fear that clients would feel uncomfortable, even though clients don't seem to care."

Ayesha, a Muslim woman who wore a hijab, embraced the rules in her job at a food processing company. She took off her hijab, highlighted her hair, put on light makeup, and wore sleeveless sheath dresses to mirror her coworkers. Not once was she asked, "Where are you from?" and "Yeah, but where are you *really* from?" unlike her sister, Khatija, who wore her hijab to her paralegal job and was asked this question all the time. But Ayesha's choice wasn't without its sacrifices, either; some of her religious family members and friends questioned her clothing decisions.

While Avery and Ayesha show that it's possible to either embrace the rules or reject the rules, many professionals I have met took a third approach: they bent the rules. These professionals met their coworkers partway—embracing the rules that required only a superficial sacrifice, but rejecting those that compromised their values. Sometimes this strategy involved compromising in the beginning, then pushing the boundaries and showing more of their authentic selves as they established their competence, commitment, and compatibility.

This was the strategy of Ngozi, a Black woman engineer. After Ngozi looked up her new coworkers online and found out that they were all white men, she straightened her hair before her first day. Then, four months in, she showed her authentic self. Here's what Ngozi told me: "Showing up with my natural Afro was like ripping off a Band-Aid. Everyone was like, 'Wow! Where did that come from?' But because I had built enough trust, the 'wow' was a 'Wow, I didn't know about this other side of you' rather than a 'Wow, you definitely don't belong here.'"

Although Ngozi was willing to compromise on her physical appearance at first, she was not willing to compromise on her name. Any time Ngozi introduced herself, her coworkers would ask, "Do you have a nickname?" When she said no, several of her coworkers offered nicknames of their own: "What about Nora? Nina? Nosy?"

"No," Ngozi insisted in the politest but firmest voice she could find. "I only go by Ngozi, like en-goh-zee."

Before long, her coworkers adapted—and her name was never questioned again.

Jomo, a Black man in an all-white team, also bent the rules, but with his clothes: "I kept seeing the same preppy look: button-downs, loafers with no-show socks, cropped chinos that show your ankles. That just wasn't me. So I decided, you know what? I'll meet you at the level you're playing at, which is smart casual. But I'm going to do it my way, which means jeans and Timbys [Timberland boots]. I wore a dress shirt to get on their level, but I wore a chain inside that I was not afraid to show off. This was my way of keeping my sense of self—of standing out while fitting in."

Remember: there are no right or wrong answers—only personal values. These personal values come together to inform a single question: what aspects of yourself are you willing—and not willing—to negotiate? Answering this question requires understanding yourself.

To help you figure it out, imagine three concentric circles. The innermost circle is the "sacred zone." This region represents your core values and identity. The next circle is the "negotiable zone." This region represents the things you care about but could sacrifice depending on the circumstances. The outermost circle is the "indifferent zone." This region represents all of the things you don't care about and could abandon without missing anything. Figure 6-2 shows what these circles look like.

FIGURE 6-2

How to decide whether to reject, bend, or embrace the rules

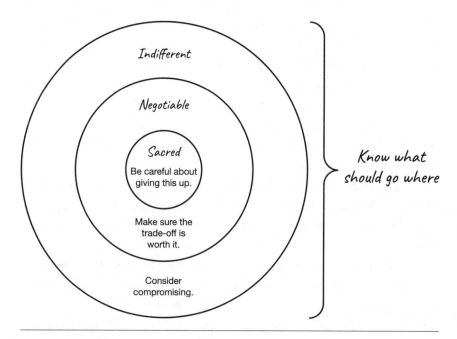

Try placing elements of your own life into these three categories. Then use what you put into each category to inform your choices. Consider giving away the elements that you are indifferent about. Carefully evaluate what you gain by giving up, or not giving up, the negotiable elements. Lastly, regularly evaluate whether you are giving up anything that might be sacred. If you are, ask yourself, What are the pros and cons—and do the benefits outweigh the costs?

Different people will put different elements inside of each circle. Avery put much of their look in the sacred zone. Ayesha put much of her look in the negotiable and indifferent zones, unlike her sister, Khatija. Ngozi put her name in the sacred zone, but her hair in the negotiable zone. Jomo had some elements of his physical appearance in the sacred zone and others in the negotiable zone. It's not that Avery, Ayesha, Khatija, Ngozi, and Jomo made the right choice and those who choose differently are wrong; it's that they made the right choice for themselves, given their personal zones of tolerance.

A word of caution: this is a hard exercise—not only because it requires digging deep within yourself but also because it can take some guesswork. Just as it is possible to undershoot the zone of compatibility, the opposite is possible too. You can overthink your look, only to find yourself adapting to something that your coworkers either didn't care about or hadn't considered carefully. Consider asking your manager, "I know it's important to _____, but I was thinking of _____ because of _____. Would it be appropriate for me to _____?" You might be pleasantly surprised by where you can reach a compromise—or not need to compromise at all.

Don't suffer silently. When in doubt, consider approaching a coworker with a shared identity and saying, "I couldn't help but notice that we're both _____. I'd love your advice on how you've been able to navigate _____. Would you have a few minutes to chat?" If there isn't such a person within your team, search your organization's directory for people on other teams. You could also reach out to leaders of employee resource groups, employee networks, or affinity groups, if your organization has them—these are people who have volunteered to support individuals from their background or identity. Consider looking outside your organization as well by going online and searching for your identity (e.g., "Asian," "woman," "LGBTQ+") + your field (e.g., "computer science," "law," "sales") + "network," "association," "conference," "circle," "union," "guild," or "alliance." It can be easy to feel alone. You aren't.

Your early career is a chance to learn about yourself, what you care about, and what you don't care about. Commitment and compatibility have their limits. As important as it may be to navigate to the intersection of the Three Cs, it is just as important to ask yourself whether you even want to go there. After all, the C of commitment stands for "Are you excited to be here?" You can fake excitement—to a point. But do you really want to? The C of compatibility stands for "Do you get along with us?" You can also fake harmony to a point. But, again, do you really want to? Luisa, who quit her administrative assistant job to work in food service, told me: "It's hard to go through life with the mindset of 'I'm never going to change.' Life is about being adaptable. Traveling with friends requires compromise. Marriage requires compromise. Teamwork requires compromise. I'm not saying 'don't change.' I'm saying that when you get to a point where you can't even be yourself, it's time to go."

What happened with Luisa?

"People gave me all these dirty looks when they heard my loud laugh and saw my tattoos, heavy makeup, and thick eyebrows," Luisa told me. "I've had managers crack jokes about how I was from the hood, then do the prison pose in front of me. I didn't want to be all proper like them in the first place. They had no personality."

Remember: there are no right or wrong answers—only personal values. Live up to your own expectations—not to the expectations others have of you.

If you found this chapter relevant, I hope that you will use the trust you build at your company to level the playing field for those coming after you. And if this chapter wasn't relevant to you because you naturally "fit" with your team, know that you have a responsibility to be an ally and to lift up those for whom "fit" comes less easily. Our uniqueness makes us who we are. Let's celebrate that fact.

Try This

- Consider what impressions your appearance will give your managers, coworkers, clients, and partners.

- Make deliberate choices about your clothes, accessories, and grooming.

- Recognize patterns in others' appearance choices and use them as a starting point when deciding on your own appearance.

- Figure out when you should reject the rules, embrace the rules, or bend the rules.

- Decide for yourself what you consider sacred, negotiable, and indifferent when it comes to your appearance.

Send the Right Signals

N eel, a management consultant, was working on a presentation for a client meeting at 2:30 p.m.—just fifteen minutes away. His manager, one of the firm's directors, and the client's CEO would all be there.

Neel sped through the remaining slides to incorporate his manager's last-minute comments, then checked the time again: 2:29 p.m. He saved the presentation and looked for the meeting invitation link, but couldn't find it. He messaged a colleague:

> Hey, do you have the invite?

Neel could hear each second ticking by in his head as he waited. The clock turned to 2:30. Then 2:31. He messaged another coworker, who immediately sent the invite. He clicked the meeting link. A pop-up window appeared: *Update required. Please update to continue.* After installing the update and restarting his computer, Neel finally entered the meeting. At 2:42 p.m.

The director finished distracting the clients. "All right, shall we get started? Neel, take it away." As Neel clicked Share Screen, his slideshow crashed. *Ughh!* He grunted and banged on his keyboard.

"Everything OK there?" the partner asked sharply.

Know This

- Everything you do and don't do can impact others' perceptions of your competence, commitment, and compatibility.

- Managing misunderstandings is all about understanding your intent and controlling your impact.

- Make sure you show the appropriate amount of urgency and seriousness.

"Ye . . . yes," Neel stammered. He had forgotten to put himself on mute. A minute later, he had the slideshow rebooted.

In the end, the clients were impressed by Neel's analysis. Six months later, though, Neel found that his end-of-project evaluation said, "Neel was easily and visibly frustrated by small issues. This behavior demonstrates a lack of awareness given that clients were present, and raises the concern of the behavior he would show if placed in more stressful situations."

What happened? Despite Neel's desire to deliver a polished presentation, what others saw was him not showing up on time (so they doubted his commitment), losing his cool in the face of a seemingly minor issue (so they doubted his competence), and behaving unprofessionally in front of clients (so they doubted his compatibility).

Neel had positive intent, but negative impact. *Intent* is what you mean. *Impact* is how you come across to other people. You know your intent; others do not. This is how misunderstandings arise.

Neel's struggles weren't entirely his fault, especially since it was his manager's last-minute changes that led to Neel scrambling in the first place. But no one else knew that. This will be true for you, too.

Remote work makes managing your impact even more challenging. All others can do is infer your intent based on what they read from you via email, hear from you via phone or voice mail, or hear and see from you via video chat. And if you never get to meet your coworkers in person, what you show in the digital world isn't just your first impression; it becomes your only impression.

Since others' perceptions of you can be unforgiving and enduring, it's important to send the right signals—that you are competent in your role, committed to the organization, and compatible with your team. Let's walk through the most common areas where people send mixed signals—and how you can avoid planting any seeds of doubt.

Emails and Instant Messages

Every email you send is a new opportunity to demonstrate your Three Cs. But because different people have different standards, it's important to know your audience—and to tailor your signals accordingly. Doing so begins with understanding your team's email and instant message (IM) culture.

Workplaces come in two general flavors:

Email-first. People in email-first workplaces grew up writing emails at work, so they send proper emails by default and text or instant message only when they need to reach someone for a quick or casual chat. Often, these workplaces are traditional white-collar settings where people have desk jobs and wear business casual or business formal.

IM-first. People in IM-first workplaces grew up casually IMing their coworkers, so they IM by default and send professional emails only when they need to communicate with an outside party or send something official. Often, these workplaces are startups or settings that don't involve a computer, like service or trades work—jobs where people wear smart casual, casual, or a uniform.

Writing at work is therefore like dressing up for work. People in email-first teams dress in business formal or business casual, then occasionally tone it down—and do the same thing with their writing. People in IM-first teams dress in smart casual or casual, then occasionally dial it up—and do the same with their writing. Like dressing for work, picking the right level of formality can mean the difference between looking like an insider and looking like an outsider.

Since formality is the common thread here, let's define "business formal," then tone down the professionalism one step at a time to explain the entire range of formalities.

Consider the following "business formal" email, which you will most frequently see in email-first organizations.

Subject: By 8/16: Draft workplan for your review
To: Bob
CC: Khatchig
Attachment: ABC workplan v3 - 2020-08-10.docx; ABC workplan v3 - 2020-08-10.pdf

Dear Bob,

Hope all is well.

Please find attached the latest project workplan for your review (Word version if you want to make track changes; PDF version if you are reviewing on mobile).

We will be sharing it with Sruthi on Tue 8/17, so it would be great to get your feedback by Mon 8/16 at 12 p.m.

Let me know if you have questions or would like to chat live. My availability is as follows:

- Tue 8/11: before 10 a.m., after 11 a.m.

- Wed 8/12: any time

- Thu 8/13: after 2 p.m.

- Fri 8/14: before 12 p.m., after 3 p.m.

Best,

Lauren

As seen in this example, you'll find a few elements in most professional emails.

- A professional salutation like "Dear," followed by an occupational honorific if applicable (e.g., Dr. or Professor) or maybe a cultural honorific (e.g., Mr., Datuk, Mme, -san), and then a first or last name, depending on the country. (Search online for your country + "working culture" and "honorifics" if you are unsure; in the United States, people typically call others by their first name except when using an honorific.)

- A greeting like "Hope you are doing well" or "Hope all is well."

- A professional sign-off like "Best," "Regards," "Sincerely," "Sincerely yours," or "Thank you."

- The primary audience of the email in the To line, people who are being kept informed in the CC line, and, if relevant, people who should receive the email but remain invisible in the BCC line.

- Writing that is clear, polite, and direct in both the subject line and the email body.

- All of the relevant details the reader will need.

- Perfect spelling, grammar, spacing, and formatting.

- No exclamation marks, emojis, or GIFs.

To "dress down" from business formal writing to business casual, simply change the greeting to "Hi," "Hello," "Good morning," "Good afternoon," or just the person's name. You can also make your sign-off more casual, with "Thanks," "Thanks so much," "Have a nice week," "Talk soon," or "Looking forward to hearing from you." You may notice that once an email thread is started, people do away with the greetings and sign-offs.

To dress down from business casual to smart casual, change the greeting to "Hey." Some people also like the sign-off "Cheers" or "Thanks!" In smart casual writing you might also see exclamation marks or emojis (typically a smiley face). To dress down from smart casual to casual, sprinkle in some exclamation marks, LOLs, emojis, or even GIFs.

The formality of IMs mirrors the formality of emails. At the business formal end, some people will write IMs like they do emails—complete with "Dear" and "Best." You'll see this behavior most often at traditional organizations where people embrace the quick side of IMs but not the casual side. Once you move to business casual writing, people might remove all greetings. The closer you get to the casual end of the spectrum, the more exclamation marks, LOLs, emojis, and GIFs you can expect to see.

To ensure that you are sending the right signals, consider rereading your writing aloud and thinking about how it will sound from the recipient's point of view. You could also ask yourself five questions before clicking Send:

Is my email free of typos and formatting inconsistencies?

People might be more forgiving of typos, incorrect numbers, multiple font types, or spacing inconsistencies if you work in a job that that doesn't require much writing (or if you are high up in the organization and have the leverage to break the rules). But it's harder to trust a new paralegal or finance analyst who forgets a "not" in a sentence. What matters in these jobs is attention to detail, so an email with typos isn't good enough. Be especially careful with people's names. Triple-check names before hitting Send.

Am I fully caught up on what's going on?

Have you skimmed your inbox to make sure you are replying to the most recent message? Have you scrolled to the start of the email thread to check that you are making a comment that adds to the discussion? Have you done what you said you'd do for your email recipient since your last exchange? These subtle actions can signal that you are organized and up to date, rather than careless and forgetful.

Am I sending this email at the appropriate time?

Is your email arriving at midnight because you are working extra late— or because you don't have your work under control? Are you waiting a week to reply because you are busy or because you don't care? To minimize any chance of doubt, try to reply as promptly as possible, mirror the urgency of others, or give a reasonable explanation for any delay. Given how easy it can be to hit Send prematurely, consider filling in your To, CC, and BCC lines only when you are ready to send your email, and typing IMs to important people in a separate window, then pasting your text into the chat.

Does the tone of my email or IM align with my intent?

Anger, frustration, or passive-aggressiveness can slip into your writing when work gets tough. Sometimes, it may be your intent to convey these emotions. Other times, you'd rather look patient and cordial. If you feel upset as you write something, consider hitting Save instead of Send and taking a walk, or waiting until the following day to finish it. If your email or IM can be interpreted in multiple ways, consider revising your note, clarifying your intent, or calling the other person instead.

Would I mind if this email or IM were forwarded to the entire team?

Emails and IMs may be convenient, but they are also permanent. And someone can easily forward or take a screenshot of them. If there is any information that you'd rather no one know besides your recipient, cover your ass (also known as CYA—which is, by the way, a real term from the world of work) and consider scheduling a phone call instead.

Phone Calls

Speaking with someone on the phone can feel like dancing with a partner. When it goes well, the performance can look and feel graceful and effortless. When it doesn't go well, all you see is people stepping over and yanking at each other. Let's focus on five effective ways to help you pull off a graceful dance:

- **Minimize background noise.** Consider taking calls from a quiet space with good reception, turning off all notification sounds, and putting yourself on mute when not speaking (especially on group calls). This can prevent people from being distracted—and wondering if the noise means you aren't taking this call seriously.

- **Be on time.** If others are calling you, stay by your phone so that you pick up on their first attempt. If you are calling others, call when you said you would, and if you can't, give others advance notice. This can prevent people from wondering whether you don't respect their time or have bad time management skills.

- **Be polite.** Consider answering calls with "Hello, this is [your name]," asking "Is now still a good time?" when calling others, ending with "Bye," and waiting a second before hanging up. This can prevent people from thinking you are too casual or disrespectful.

- **Keep it smooth.** If you tend to cut others off, try waiting half a second after someone finishes speaking to start speaking yourself. If you tend to blank out and don't know what to say next, try coming up with your response as others are still speaking, while still listening to the other person. This can prevent people from feeling that you either aren't listening or are not interested in the conversation.

- **Pause.** Consider pausing occasionally when making a string of long points, to allow others to contribute and to help you balance your speaking time. This can prevent people from wondering if you're talking so much because you are excited or because you like the sound of your own voice.

Of course, it's not realistic to take all these steps all the time. When you must be late or take a call from a noisy place, offer reasonable explanations, whether it's "Sorry, my last meeting went over" or "There's construction outside my house and there's nowhere else I can take this call." To play it safe, consider acknowledging that you know you've violated an unspoken rule. That way people will know what you consider acceptable and unacceptable behavior. Always clarify things that people can misinterpret. You never know how far people's minds might wander.

No one's perfect, of course. In fact, anyone who tells you that they've never taken a call from the bathroom is lying to you. It all depends on the situation and how much authority you have for calling the shots and bending the rules. A senior manager at a digital marketing agency told me, "At my company we all follow the rules when we are meeting with clients—when we really care about the audience. But for meetings that people don't care about? People do all sorts of things. One of my bosses cooked a full lunch and dinner during a call."

In short, we all get lazy. Or sick of following the rules. But sometimes you need to know—and embrace—the rules to earn the right to strategically break them.

Video Calls

With video calls you are sending your audience two signals: an audio signal of whatever others can hear from you and a visual signal of whatever others can see in your video chat window. The audio tips we discussed under the phone calls section still apply here, so we won't repeat them. Let's instead discuss how you can send the right signals through video.

Be mindful of your background

For any object that is visible in your video chat window, ask yourself: *What signal is this sending to my audience?* Might colleagues see you working in bed and wonder if you are alternating between working and napping? Might they see people behind you and assume you are socializing or distracted? Unless there is a certain statement you want to make with an image or object, try for a plain wall, bookshelf, or room divider and avoid leaving room for people to walk behind you.

Be mindful of your upper-body appearance

When it comes to upper-body clothing or grooming, ask yourself: *Am I dressed at the same level as coworkers with my identity and seniority?* Some people dress down to casual when working remotely, even if they typically wear business casual. Others retain their same look. Still others dress casually with insiders but formally with outsiders. When choosing between looks, consider picking the more formal option. If you expect to stand up during the video call, either look presentable below the waist or turn off your video before standing up.

Be mindful of your actions

For anything you do while the camera is on, ask yourself: *Might I look distracted?* If you are multitasking, be careful about what your moving eyes or the reflection in your glasses might reveal. Although drinking on camera is fine (water or coffee, at least!), eating often isn't, so mirror others at your level. If there is a chance that your taking notes can be mistaken for your not paying attention, consider clarifying with a remark like, "Let me write this down." If you must step out, consider turning off your video for a moment.

Be mindful of what you share on-screen

With anything that might show up when your screen is shared, ask yourself: *Might this make me look distracted or unprofessional?* Be mindful of your desktop folders, browser tabs, browser favorites, minimized windows, and taskbar icons. Consider disabling all notifications and pop-up windows before you share your screen. Consistency is important: you want what people see to align with what you are saying. Having a "20% off!" promotional email on your screen in the middle of a serious presentation doesn't quite do that.

Be mindful of what you'll need to do during the meeting

Before joining a meeting, ask yourself: *Is there anything I might need to refer to, share on-screen, send, or coordinate?* If so, consider having all the files open and draft emails queued up—and doing a test run before the meeting. That way, you know exactly where to click and can avoid scrambling to figure things out in front of everyone.

Voice Mails

Voice mails are quickly falling out of favor as people opt to email or instant message others instead. That said, they are still important to get right, especially since the people you will need to leave voice mails for are probably more-traditional folks who value professionalism. Luckily, voice mails are relatively straightforward. Simply use the following script:

> Hi [_Lance_]. This is [_Gorick Ng_] calling from [_Acme Corporation_]. Hope you're doing well. It is [_Monday, August 17th, at 10 a.m._]. I wanted to give you a call to [_discuss the latest contract_]. Please call me back when you have a moment. I should be free until [_1 p.m. Pacific Time_]. My number here is [_617-123-4567_]. Once again, it's [_617-123-4567_]. Thank you so much.

And if you are setting up your own phone's voice mail greeting, here is a standard professional greeting to consider:

> Hi. You've reached the voice mail of [_Gorick Ng_]. Sorry I am unable to take your call at this moment. Please leave your name, number, and a brief message and I will get back to you as soon as I can. Thank you and have a nice day.

Since the point of voice mails and voice mail greetings is simply to get your point across, there typically isn't much creativity involved. But because they are so short, it's important to send the right signal—that you are professional and courteous. So, get to the point, enunciate every word clearly, and be sure there isn't any noise in the background.

Online Activity

Your online activity is an extension of you. People are watching, people are noticing, and people are judging. It's important to make sure that there is consistency between the signals you send in the digital world and those you send in the physical world. Here are some digital signals to be aware of:

- Your social media posts, likes, and shares—which others can use to judge where you are and what you are up to

- Your activity on your employer-issued device(s)—which your IT department can use to judge how you are using company time

- Your status on instant messenger—which your coworkers can use to judge when you are online, offline, and busy

- Your calendar entries that are public—which your teammates can use to judge what you are doing day-to-day

- Your file version numbers, time stamps, and track changes, and whose name is on the file—which others can use to judge when, how hard, and how quickly you are working and who did the work

- Your email or messenger read receipts—which others can use to judge if you are around (and perhaps ignoring them)

- Your email threads when you forward long messages—which others can use to judge how you communicate with people

Since there are so many possible digital signals—and so many ways they may be misinterpreted—the idea isn't to be paranoid and not live your life. It's to be mindful that, for example, it is now the norm for recruiters to search online for job candidates, employees to search for their coworkers, and clients to search for their service providers. And internally, even if colleagues aren't deliberately looking for information about you, they are presented with plenty of your digital signals. So, before hitting Send or Post, ask yourself: How might this come across to others? Will I regret this signal days, weeks, months, or years from now?

In-Person Behavior

While you might be able to shield yourself behind your laptop or phone when working remotely, there are fewer places to hide when you are working in person. As a high school department head told me, "You need to assume that you are always being watched." Even the tiniest of gestures can make a big impression.

No matter if you are handling students or spreadsheets, reporting to a parent or a director, or working in a home or on a construction site, it's important to check in on yourself. Here are some questions to consider:

- When and how do you arrive at and leave work—and what does it say about your time management abilities and commitment?

- What do you leave on your desk, in your trash can, and in the printer—and what does it say about your priorities?

- How are your table manners when eating meals with others—and what does it say about how respectful you are of the culture you are in?

- How visible are you at work—and what does it say about how hard you are working?

- How loudly do you discuss confidential information—and what does it say about your ability to keep secrets?

The list is endless. The bottom line is this: everything you do, and don't do, in person can send a signal. Make sure the signals you send are the ones you want to be remembered for.

In the end, sending the right signals comes down to showing the right amount of urgency and seriousness. But there's a challenge: people are comparing you not to some objective standard but to their personal definitions of "urgent" and "serious." And those personal definitions are shaped over years by one's own culture, training, working style, and personality.

One way to determine which signals you may want to prioritize sending is to analyze how *monochronic* or *polychronic* your company's work culture is.[1] Do your coworkers and clients tend to block off specific times for specific activities and stay on schedule? If so, they might lean more toward the monochronic end of the spectrum, and see time as something to be divided into blocks and organized. Do your coworkers and clients tend to multitask, change their plans, and go with the flow? If so, they might lean more toward the polychronic end of the spectrum, and see time as more fluid and less tangible. Table 7-1 shows a few more differences between these two types of people.

This distinction is important because monochronic people (monochrons) might see polychronic people (polychrons) as disengaged,

TABLE 7-1

How to distinguish between monochronic and polychronic people

Monochronic people	Polychronic people
Do one thing at a time	Do many things at a time
See interruptions as bad	See interruptions as normal
Take deadlines as orders	Take deadlines as suggestions
Prioritize getting the job done	Prioritize building relationships
Rarely change plans	Frequently change plans
Are prompt no matter what	Are prompt depending on the relationship
Build short-term relationships	Build long-term relationships

Source: Adapted from Giancarlo Duranti and Olvers Di Prata, "Everything Is About Time: Does It Have the Same Meaning All Over the World?" (paper presented at the PMI Global Congress, Amsterdam, the Netherlands, 2009).

disorganized, or lazy, even though polychrons might simply be more used to multitasking or working with looser deadlines and commitments. Meanwhile, polychrons might see monochrons as uptight, demanding, or disrespectful, even though monochrons might be trying to respect the other person's time by working quickly and efficiently. This was the lesson that Cici, a chief of staff at an agriculture company who moved from New York to Zambia, learned the hard way. According to Cici's manager:

> Cici was only doing what she was trained to do, but her relentless push for output from managers was perceived as badgering and disrespectful. I would often hear from the C-suite, "Can you please tell your girl to slow her roll? This is Lusaka, not New York!" The fast-paced consulting disciplines of New York were totally at odds with the laid-back, "problems solve themselves" culture of Zambia. Zambian culture is passive-aggressive and subtle. There are few cues to signal you're driving off a cliff until it's too late.

In other words, there isn't a universal standard for positive signals. It all depends on your audience. If you are among people who see time in the same way you do, then feel free to retain your natural working style.

But if you are a polychron among monochrons, then you might want to send signals that include being on time, responding promptly, and single-tasking in the presence of others. And if you are a monochron among polychrons, then consider taking a closer look at whether the signals you are sending might be seen as too serious or intense. Instead of responding right away, consider mirroring the urgency of others. Instead of imposing strict "do X by Y time" deadlines, consider pushing more gently and getting comfortable with shifting timelines and being told you'll get an answer "soon." Polychronism and monochronism aside, expect others' backgrounds and circumstances to guide their hidden expectations of you. Might your manager be a workaholic? Expect higher standards for signals that speak to your productivity. Might they have family or other commitments outside of work? Expect greater forgiveness for signals that show that you value work-life balance. Might they not care much for professionalism? Expect to throw out some, or even most, of the expectations in this chapter. Be kind to yourself. We all make mistakes. And when it comes to signals, your "mistake" may not be a mistake per se; it may be that you just didn't follow your colleagues' way of doing things. Recognize patterns—and be more deliberate about your urgency and seriousness next time. You may need to work on your impact, but at least you know that your intent is in the right place. You're already halfway there.

Try This

- Be mindful of the impression you make through your emails, instant messages, phone calls, voice mails, video calls, online activities, and in-person behavior.

- Show the right dose of urgency and seriousness by toning down your intensity (when among polychrons) or being more prompt and structured (when among monochrons).

- Regularly ask yourself, What signals am I sending?

SECRETS TO

GETTING THE
JOB DONE

Take Ownership

Assignments in school are unlike assignments in the workplace. In school, they come with clear instructions and explicit grading rubrics. In the workplace, your instructions might be your manager rambling in a meeting or forwarding you a long email thread and asking, "Can you follow up?" In school, deadlines are both written and spoken. In the workplace, deadlines are often unwritten and unspoken. If you aren't careful, it can be easy to get overwhelmed. To ensure that you stay sane and become the most competent professional you can be, it helps to be deliberate.

Understand Your Assignments

Once you receive a task, one of the most important things you can do is ask yourself, Is there anything I'm unclear about? Despite their good intentions, managers often tell you only a fraction of what you need to know. They may simply forget to tell you the rest, assume you know something already, or think that certain information was not important enough to share.

If not clarified, these missing details can mean you do the wrong work and even look incompetent. The appropriate time to ask for clarification is, therefore, immediately—and not five minutes from now, when your manager has moved on to something else. To ensure that you leave nothing ambiguous, take the following steps.

Know This

- The secret to doing a good job is to understand what is expected of you and to stay one step ahead of your boss.

- The easier you make it for others to help you, the more likely you'll be helped.

- Don't be afraid to manage your manager.

See the big picture

Behind every task is a goal. If you are asked to buy a cake, the *task* may be to buy a cake, but the *goal* is broader than that. Maybe the cake is for a coworker's birthday; maybe it's for someone's retirement; maybe it's a prop for a photo shoot. If you don't first understand why the task exists, you may end up overlooking the candles for the birthday cake, the farewell note for the retirement, or the desired type of cake for the photo shoot.

To understand the broader goal, consider asking questions like, "What is this for?" "What's the broader objective?" "What does success look like?" or "Who is the audience?" Once you start working, keep reminding yourself of the broader goal. If something you're doing doesn't help achieve the goal or solve the problem, then it may be worthwhile to return to your manager and say, "I was thinking about our goal of _____ and was wondering if it might make more sense to do _____ instead of _____. What do you think?" This can be a subtle but effective way to remind people of your competence—and to avoid wasting your time on work that doesn't matter.

Understand what, how, and by when

Whenever you are assigned a task, there are three questions you need to answer with your manager: What do I need to do? How should I do it? And by when do I need to get it done? If you don't have answers to all three questions, try to clarify immediately; otherwise, you will do the wrong work, do it the wrong way, or do it too late—and tarnish your image of competence. It may be that your manager forgot to tell you something. Or, perhaps they hadn't considered these details and are relying on you to manage the process. And if your manager gives you rambling, incoherent answers, they might need you to manage them through the ambiguity, in which case try the following:

If your manager isn't clear on *what* or *how*, try asking them or a colleague what's been tried before. Or look through internal files or the internet to find templates or examples. Compare the options, pick the one you like best, and then show the options to your manager with a comment like, "We could try some version of _____, _____, or _____. I suggest we go with _____, but change _____ because of _____. Do you agree?" (A quick caution on the how: If this is the first time you are doing something, consider asking, "Is there a certain process, method, or template I should follow?" You may be expected to follow some standard process, especially if you work in a bureaucratic organization where everyone has their own defined tasks and there is a certain way of doing everything.)

If your manager isn't clear on *by when*, try assessing how polychronic or monochronic your coworkers are (see chapter 7 for what this is about) and mirroring their urgency, gauging how urgent and important the task is compared to other tasks that you've been assigned, identifying when colleagues will need to use your work, or asking "When would you like to check in?"

Don't be fooled: if your manager says, "We'll figure it out," chances are they don't mean "We will figure it out." They probably mean "*You* will figure it out." They are relying on you to help them turn the ambiguous into the unambiguous.

Understand RACI

Behind every assignment is a hidden acronym that the professional world calls RACI (pronounced "racy"). Each letter stands for how someone relates to a project: *responsible* for doing the work, *accountable* for the success of the work, needs to be *consulted* on the work, and needs to be *informed* on the status of the work.

You'll hear the word "accountable" a lot in the workplace. It is simply a fancy word to say "having your reputation on the line in the event that something goes wrong." So you might be responsible for a project, but your manager is accountable for the project's success. This means that if you make a mistake, your manager is partly to blame because they should have done a better job checking your work. Just because your manager is accountable doesn't mean you can't be as well, though. High performers treat every assignment as if it were their reputations—not their manager's—that are on the line. In fact, this is what taking owner-ship—the focus of this chapter—is all about.

The key to using RACI is to clarify what each letter in the acronym refers to in your project before you start. To clarify who's responsible, try asking, "Is there anyone else I should be working with?" and "Who is responsible for what?" To clarify who's accountable, try asking, "Who needs to sign off on this work?" To clarify who needs to be consulted, try asking, "Is there anyone else whose perspective I should get?" To clarify who needs to be informed, try asking, "Is there anyone else I should keep up to date?"

Managing the expectations of each person represented by RACI is important for your competence and compatibility. Otherwise, someone who should be consulted or kept informed might see you as overbearing or threatening if you don't ask for their opinion (even if you didn't know you needed to). This can be especially important when you are working re-motely and can't see your manager dropping by someone's desk—and so you can't tell who should or should not be involved in a certain decision.

Think multiple steps ahead

Picture yourself doing each step of your assignment from start to finish. What logins will you need? Who will you need to talk to? What analyses will you need to conduct? Then, ask yourself:

- Do I understand how to do each step of the task?

- Do I have everything I need to get started?

- Am I being asked to do something that contradicts or conflicts with something else I've been told to do?

Nothing is too basic or too obvious to clarify. People might assume that you have access to something you don't, or that something is quick and easy when it isn't. You might assume that something is time-consuming and complicated when it should not be. If you have even the slightest amount of doubt, be proactive and ask. Spending an extra thirty seconds clarifying something up front could save you thirty hours later.

Work backward from the deadline

In the workplace, if a task has a deadline, it typically has two or more deadlines: a *final* deadline (which is often the one you'll hear about) and at least one *interim* deadline (which is usually unspoken). The final deadline is when something will be released, published, or sent out. The interim deadline is an internal check-in to make sure that you are on track (and that the relevant people in your RACI list are happy). Often, you'll want to ask for at least one interim deadline shortly after your first meeting. Here are some ways to ask the question:

"When should we check in for me to provide a status update?"

"How about we check in as soon as I put an outline together?"

"Would it make sense for us to check in tomorrow to make sure I am on track?"

"This is my first time doing this. How about I give it a shot, then give you a status update by the end of the day?"

If your work is digital, consider sharing your work the day before your check-in to give your manager time to review. Then, at the meeting, ask, "Am I on track?" And if your status update doesn't require a discussion, your check-in may just be a simple email to your manager with your draft, outline, mock-up, sketch, or first attempt. Once your manager says "This looks good!" you can continue with the assurance that you are on the right track, your manager hasn't changed their mind, and you aren't wasting your time.

Beyond that first check-in, it is also important to look and think ahead. If you were assigned a task on Wednesday, October 1, and it's due on Friday, October 10, it may seem like you have seven weekdays to finish. But

FIGURE 8-1

How to work backward from the deadline

Actual deadline
(unless everyone is OK
working over the weekend)

Two days to finish
(first draft), not seven!

Sunday	Monday	Tuesday	Wednesday	Thursday	Friday	Saturday
			1 Today	2	3	4
5	6 Manager away	7	8 Manager's manager away	9	10 Client meeting	

Two-day window
to get approval from
manager's manager

Last chance to
finalize everything

Final deadline
(but really October 9
should be the final deadline
so we aren't scrambling
on meeting day)

consider other relevant factors: if your manager (who needs to review the work) will be away the following Monday and your manager's manager (who needs to approve the work) will be away the following Wednesday, then you may not have seven weekdays for your first draft—you may have just two days. Figure 8-1 shows how to work backward from your final deadline to plan out your interim deadlines.

If you notice such conflicts, consider alerting others with a statement like, "I know you'll be away on Monday, so how about we meet on Friday of this week?" Remembering for your manager is a subtle but effective way to signal, "Hey, don't worry. I've got things under control."

In jobs where people freely share their calendars, some managers may even expect you to peek at their calendars before scheduling meetings. Consider pulling up their calendar with them present so you can find a time immediately—and so your manager can say, "Oops, I actually have something booked then that I haven't put into my calendar." Mediocre performers wait for their managers to manage them. High performers manage their managers.

Repeat it back

What you think you heard may not always reflect what others said—or thought they said. To minimize the odds of misunderstanding, consider repeating back what you think you heard and giving others the chance to correct you. Here are a few options:

"Just to play back what I think I heard: _____. Is that correct?"

"In terms of next steps, I will _____, right?"

"I will do _____ by _____ time and use _____ method. How does that sound?"

"OK, I will _____ and then _____. Let me know if I am missing anything."

"I was thinking I would _____. Would that work?"

Although simply repeating back what you heard is often good enough, if your manager is forgetful, if you are working in a group, or if chaos would erupt if anyone misremembered the details (like if you are editing a contract for a negotiation), you may need to cover your ass (CYA), so don't just repeat back what you heard; write it in an email to everyone involved.

Squash Any Problems

Once you start doing your job, you may end up having questions, encountering problems, facing conflicts, or experiencing a sudden change of plans. In these moments it can be easy to get worried and feel like something was your fault. Often, it isn't. These aren't situations to dread or avoid; they're opportunities for you to prove how competent you are at managing expectations, people, and ambiguity. Here are some strategies for addressing any problem, questions, or changes of plans.

If you have questions, bundle, escalate, and show your homework

When you have a nonurgent question, remember the rule of *do—and show—your homework*. Start by searching your email and browsing any

FIGURE 8-2

How to ask questions at work

Ask your manager's manager

Ask your manager

Ask another coworker

Ask a junior coworker

Search online

Browse internal files

Bundle questions

shared folders. Then search online. If you can't find the answer, bundle and escalate: collect a bunch of questions and bring them to a coworker at your level when they don't look busy or someone whose job is to answer your specific question (e.g., HR or IT). If they can't help you either, ask the next most appropriate person, followed by your manager, followed by your manager's manager. Like climbing a ladder, go up one rung at a time. Figure 8-2 shows how to think about climbing the ladder.

Each time you approach someone with your bundle of questions, explain the context and show your homework. Instead of asking, "How do I log in to the enterprise resource planning system?" try, "How do I log in to the enterprise resource planning system? I'm trying to pull some data for my analysis. I tried looking in the onboarding checklist but couldn't find it. It doesn't seem like Ken has access either." The idea is to frame your request as "Here's my question—and here's *why* I'm asking this question." Or, "Here's what I know—and here's what I *don't* know." Figure 8-3 has five additional structures to consider trying.

FIGURE 8-3

How to show your homework when asking questions

- I'm unsure about _____ . I suspect _____ given _____ .
  this question   this is the answer   these hypotheses
  Am I on the right track?

- I couldn't find _____ despite searching _____ . Where is it?
  this thing/answer   all of these places

- I'm struggling with _____ and tried _____ , but _____ .
  these obstacles   these options   faced these issues
  What am I missing?

- I'm trying to figure out _____ , but can't find _____ . Whom should
  this problem   this thing
  I speak to?

- I know I asked this earlier, but I'm unsure about _____ , so I was
  this thing
  wondering _____ .
  if you can help/repeat what you said

To boost your compatibility, it can be helpful to explain why you think someone is the most appropriate person for your question, so they don't think you're wasting their time. It could be as simple as saying, "I heard you're the supply chain expert" or "I saw your name in the file, so I thought I'd ask you first." And to boost your competence, watch your patterns and don't let history repeat itself: If others tell you something, repeat it back, repeat it to yourself, take notes—do whatever you need to do to remember what they said. Try not to make someone need to tell you the same thing twice—and try not to have to ask the same question twice. If you have to ask again (or if you keep relying on the same person), consider trying a different person. You can also offer an acknowledgment like, "Sorry, I know we talked about this, but I can't seem to find it in my notes" or "I know I've been asking a lot of questions, but I have a few more if you wouldn't mind."

Your goal is to ask five questions at one time, not one question five separate times; show that you've done everything you can to help yourself before involving others; and show empathy for your busy coworkers. No matter how much others may want to help, they are also juggling their own responsibilities, so it is disruptive if they have to search online on your behalf, answer a question that could have been directed at someone more junior, or say the same thing over and over again.

People also can't read your mind and don't know how much you've done to help yourself, so they can't automatically give you credit for being competent and committed. The more convinced people are that you've done everything you can, the more people will think *Ah, that's reasonable* instead of *Couldn't you have figured this out yourself?*

If you aren't sure what to do next, give others something to react to

If you have any "What should I do next?" questions, resist the urge to ask for help immediately unless it is urgent. You want to send the right signal—that you can figure it out and won't stop what you're doing in the face of ambiguity. Ask yourself, *What would I do next if I "owned" this situation fully and didn't have someone else to go to for help?* Then, try taking these steps:

1. Look for examples of how others have approached similar issues or questions.

2. Brainstorm some solutions using prior examples as a starting point.

3. Compare the pros and cons of each option.

4. If you can't decide between two options, try both (if doing so is quick and easy).

5. Bundle any other questions you may have.

6. Ask for help from your coworker or manager (or ask over email/IM).

7. Show your homework by framing your question as, "I'm not sure what to do next, but I was thinking of _____ or _____. I suggest _____ because _____. Do you feel differently?"

8. Whenever possible, avoid open-ended questions like "What do you think?" because they can be time-consuming to answer. Instead, try a multiple-choice question (e.g., "Which do you prefer: A, B, or C?"), a yes-or-no question (e.g., "May I move ahead with this plan?"), a default (e.g., "I plan to do _____; let me know if you'd prefer a different approach"), a combination (e.g., "Which do you prefer: A, B, or C? I will do C unless you say otherwise"), or a combination with a deadline (e.g., "Which do you prefer: A, B, or C? I will plan to do C unless I hear from you before Monday, 8/23, at 12 p.m.").

If you are writing an email or IM, try to include a clear call to action—a statement that specifies the type of response you need. So, instead of saying, "The contract is ready for review," say, "Please sign off on the attached contract so I can send it to the team at 12 p.m. ET. I've called out all edits as track changes" or "Would it be helpful for us to meet to discuss the contract? Let me know and I will find a time" or "Let's meet to discuss the latest contract. I am free at the following times—let me know which time you'd prefer." Emails without a question mark or a "Let me know" (especially at the top) are easy to ignore. Whether it's your subject line, your call to action, your calendar invitations, or even your file names, try to leave nothing ambiguous. Table 8-1 shows how to transform ambiguous statements into unambiguous ones.

This might all seem like a lot of extra work, but these little steps can mean the difference between getting and not getting what you need. As a researcher at a think tank told me, "Managers often don't know what they want; they only know what they don't like." If you don't give others something to react to, you're setting yourself up for the dreaded question, "Uhh, I don't know . . . what do you think?"

If you need others' help, minimize others' workload

The more steps it takes for others to complete a task, the more likely they'll give up—and the less likely you'll get what you need. On the other hand, the simpler a task is, the more likely it is that people will help—and actually get it done. So, before asking for help, think multiple steps ahead and ask yourself, *What are all the steps that others will need to take to help*

TABLE 8-1

How to turn ambiguous statements into unambiguous statements

	Ambiguous	Unambiguous
Email subjects	Lunch	[By Tue. 12 noon] Submit lunch order
File names	Draft.xlsx	2021 Marketing Budget - 2020-10-25.xlsx
Scheduling requests	How about this afternoon?	Are you free after 2 p.m. today? If not, let me know some other times that work.
Email requests	I updated some numbers in the budget.	I increased the marketing line by 5% per Nate's request. Let me know if you see any issues. I will plan to submit by 4 p.m. ET today.
Calendar subjects	Catch up	Lea-Eric call re: Emerging Leaders Program
Calendar locations	Call	Vishnu to call Camille at 617-123-4567

me—and which of them can I do on their behalf ahead of time? Will others need to dig for a certain file? Consider attaching the file to your email. Will others need to look at their calendar to find an available time to meet? Consider offering your availability in their time zone. Will others need to look up a certain website? Consider including a hyperlink in your email. Make it easy for others to help you.

If you are making decisions, see the big picture and play out the consequences

Are you working on one piece of a bigger project? Are you working on something that other people will rely on? Are you looking to change anything that might affect others? If so, before making any changes, play out the scenario in your head.

For example, are you asking to take vacation time? Consider looking at your team's calendar first to make sure you won't be away when others need you (or that you have a plan for minimizing the impact of your absence). Are you changing a line of code that is related to others' work?

Consider consulting others before making your change. Are you planning to present something that might catch someone off guard? Consider sharing your presentation with that person so that they are on your side during your presentation. Be predictable. The less you surprise your coworkers, the less they will need to scramble to accommodate you. The less they need to accommodate you, the more "user-friendly" you will be as a coworker. And the more user-friendly you are as a coworker, the more compatible you will come across.

If you see a problem, be proactive and flag (or even solve) it

If you spot an error in someone's work, tell that person privately (when in doubt, praise publicly, but correct privately, unless it is not the culture of your team). It can be as simple as IMing your coworker and saying, "Hey, this might already be on your radar, but I noticed an issue with _____. Just wanted to let you know."

If you find a problem with your own work, correct it. The more significant the problem is, the more hierarchical your team is, and the more standard operating procedures (typical ways of doing things) you have in your role, the more you'll want to bring options to your manager and ask for their opinion, rather than make decisions on your own. For example, you could say, "I wanted to let you know that I noticed an issue with _____. After investigating, I discovered _____. Would it make sense for me to do _____ or _____? I'm leaning toward _____, but I wanted to check first." The more you establish a pattern of not just passing information along, but of adding your point of view, the more managers will trust your judgment and competence— and the more leeway you will be given to solve problems independently in the future.

Before long, you won't be asking, "Would it make sense for me to do _____ or _____?" Instead, you will be saying, "I plan to do _____. Let me know if you feel differently." Once your manager has full faith in your competence, you might even end up saying, "I did _____. Just wanted to let you know." It all comes down to saving your manager time and stress, and bringing solutions rather than problems.

If you receive conflicting instructions, bring the appropriate people together

Different managers may have their own opinions about the *what, how,* or *by when* of your work. If you are working with multiple managers and they rarely talk to each other, be careful—you're almost guaranteed to receive inconsistent directions that, if not managed, could lead to unnecessary stress.

If you've had a chance to ask your managers, "Would it be helpful if I CC'd both of you on major emails so we're on the same page?" then you are already on your way to preventing such a situation from happening. But if you are meeting with manager A and aren't sure if manager B might disagree with what manager A is saying, try asking manager A, "Just to make sure manager B is on board, how about I summarize our discussion in an email to her and CC you?" Or, if your managers are better at in-person conversations than emails, or if you can foresee many back-and-forth messages, consider saying, "Just to make sure we're on the same page, can I find fifteen minutes for the three of us to get together?" The goal is to avoid being stuck in the middle. It's not worth the time and stress of trying to read your managers' minds, especially since siding with one manager could upset or alienate the other one. Let them sort out their disagreements themselves.

If others help you, make them look and feel good

Don't be stingy with flattery. It's not only free—it's universally appreciated. Everyone likes to be admired, recognized, and thanked, so if you're going to someone because you trust their opinion, look to them as an expert, or admire their work, tell them. You can say something like, "I'd love to follow in your footsteps, particularly with _____" or "I really appreciate you taking the time to explain this concept to me, given how busy you are with _____." Or, in meetings, you could try statements like "Special thanks to _____ for _____" or "Shout-out to _____ for _____." These little gestures of appreciation can go a long way, especially if you are specific. You don't want to shower others with empty flattery, but if there's an opportunity to sprinkle in a thoughtful comment, be generous. Make it a habit to send a thank-you email after anyone helps you. The odds of someone getting annoyed by you thanking them are approximately 0 percent. The odds of someone getting annoyed if you disappear after they spent time helping you are approximately 100 percent.

Stay One Step Ahead of Your Boss

Finishing a task or project in the workplace is unlike finishing a homework assignment or test in school. In school, after you finish answering that question or writing that essay, all you have to do is click Submit and wait. In the workplace, finishing the task is only the second-to-last step. The last step is to figure out how to present your work to maximize others' perceptions of your competence and commitment. Before asking your manager to review what you've done, try asking yourself the following questions.

Have I followed all directions I've been given (or noted why I didn't)?

To stay above expectations, keep a list of all suggestions and changes you've received and, before sharing your work, check that list again. If there is something that you couldn't do or that wasn't feasible, share it up front with a disclaimer. Here are a few options:

> "You asked for _____, but given _____, I did _____. Let me know your thoughts."

> "I finished _____, but am still working on _____, which I expect to finish by _____."

> "Note that _____ because _____. Would you suggest a different approach?"

These can all be subtle but effective ways to manage expectations, show that you were listening, and signal that you are anticipating your manager's questions. Remember for your manager: doing so can help you build a reputation as someone who won't let promises slip just because no one's paying attention. Pro tip: open a blank document or draft email to keep a running list of points you want to make and questions you have for your manager. That way, you don't have to scramble to remember everything at the last minute. All you need to do is finish your assignment, edit your email, and click Send.

Have I focused on the details that matter?

The threshold for what's considered good enough in a given task will depend on the job you have and your context. If you are an engineer, people may not care if every pixel in your presentation is perfect as long as your math is accurate. If you are a designer, people may not care if your math is off as long as every pixel in your design is perfect. If you are presenting something to coworkers at your level, people may not care if things don't look pretty. But if you are presenting something to a higher-up or client, people likely *will* care because any formatting inconsistencies or typos reflect poorly on your team's competence. And if you are in a job like health care, engineering, construction, or logistics—where the cost of not doing things by a standard operating procedure could be death, injury, a lawsuit, a massive expense, or someone getting fired—the threshold for "good enough" is likely even higher.

To make sure you remain competent, ask yourself, *What will people scrutinize?* Recognize patterns from your coworkers—what are people looking for (and not looking for)? Where do others put their energy (and not put their energy)? Then, make sure those details are perfect before you let others see your work. Or proactively alert others that you are aware that something important is missing or isn't perfect, so there are no surprises. If you ever hear that you should show more attention to detail, your manager is trying to say that something that matters isn't quite good enough. Take a closer look at whether there might be typos, inconsistencies, miscalculations, sloppy formatting, or forgotten details in your work.

Do I have a clear call to action?

If you write a blog post for the company, share it with your team, and say something vague like "Thoughts?" the feedback you get might be equally vague: "It's too long," "I don't like the image at the top," or "The grammar is off in the second paragraph." If you were only interested in knowing whether you selected the right topic for the blog, then all of this feedback is likely to be a waste of time. To prevent others from getting distracted—and potentially giving you feedback you don't need—ask yourself: *What do I want others to focus on—and not focus on?* Then be explicit in your call to action with a question like, "I just wrote a first draft—please see attached. Is this the right topic and framing? Don't worry about formatting or grammar—I will fix it after nailing down the broad theme." Hopefully, this can also help you save some time and stress.

Have I presented my work in a way that's easy to review?

To ensure that you get the feedback you need, think about how your audience will view, edit, or comment on your work. Then try to share your work in the most user-friendly format. If your recipient needs to make edits, consider sending the raw file. If you don't know which device the recipient will view the file on, consider sending a PDF. If you're still in doubt, consider sharing both a PDF and an editable file. If a login is required, include the link and login.

Have I prepared answers to the questions my manager might ask?

Think multiple steps ahead: put yourself in the shoes of your reviewer and ask yourself, *What questions would I have if I were them?* Then either proactively address the questions in an email or IM or be ready with answers in your head. Common questions include:

"Why did you do it this way?" (Be ready to explain your thought process)

"Why didn't you include _____?" (Be ready to explain why it was omitted)

"Have you talked to _____?" (Be ready to share what you talked about)

These questions can be scary to hear, but they are your manager's way of checking to make sure that you've thought through everything. Unless your team has a standard operating procedure, often there won't be a right or wrong way of doing things. Instead, the "right" way is nothing more than one where the pros outweigh the cons. So be prepared to share the different options you considered, along with why you chose one option over another. This is your chance to show how competent you are in making the right decisions. The highest performers don't answer with "That's a good question. I haven't thought about it before." They always have a reason for why they did what they did.

Have I figured out (and shared) what I plan to do next?

Rather than just submitting your work, consider adding a note about next steps, like any of the following:

"While you review this, I'm going to shift my focus to _____."

"Based on this, would it be helpful for me to get started on _____?"

"Is there anything else you need from me?"

These can all be subtle but effective ways to signal, *I'm not here just to follow instructions; I'm here to help the team achieve its goals.* Consider it a reminder to others of your competence and commitment.

Use these lines strategically, of course. If you are being told to do something only because some higher-up wants to appease some other higher-up, you may not want to ask for more work. You may, instead, want to do a good enough job and move on with your life. What you don't want is for that higher-up to say, "Wow, that was great. Can you do this and this and this as well?" Save yourself from the misery. Know when to embrace the rules—and when to bend the rules.

I once interviewed Veronica, an intern at a hospital. Veronica had just graduated from medical school and was reporting to a resident, an experienced doctor who was training to be a specialist. It was Veronica's second week at the hospital. Like all doctors-in-training, Veronica was checking everything with her resident out of a fear of making a mistake. When a patient or nurse asked her a question she didn't know how to answer, she'd say, "Let me check for you," and then chase down her resident for help. She always made sure she was following the usual process. She was doing well. But then she was put to the test.

Veronica had a patient who was scheduled to go for surgery. But just as the patient was being wheeled to the operating floor, the anesthesiologist on the case said that he wasn't comfortable with the surgery, so he wanted to postpone the operation. Veronica, who was with another patient, received a notification on her pager. The anesthesiologist, surgeon, surgical resident, pharmacist, and nurse—people she hadn't met before—were asking to meet with a member of the medical team. Veronica's heart started pounding. She ran to her resident and explained what was happening.

"The surgery team wants to meet," Veronica said.

The resident stared back blankly. "Okay . . ."

"They want to meet *now*," Veronica clarified.

"Then why don't you go down there?" the resident said.

"Me?!"

"Yes, you. This is *your* patient, no?"

Veronica nodded slowly as it dawned on her. *This* is *my patient! I* am *a member of the team.* She rushed to the operating room and introduced herself.

"We'd advise postponing the surgery," the surgeon said. Would that be OK?" He and the anesthesiologist explained the risks.

Veronica gulped. *You're asking me to decide?* But what she said was, "Yes, this sounds like the best course of action. We all want what is best for this patient." As the words came out of her mouth, she felt herself standing taller. She wasn't the impostor she thought she was. They had treated her as an equal. It was like she was one of them.

When Veronica returned to her workstation, she did something she had never done before: she took ownership. First, she explained the surgery delay to the patient and called the patient's family to update them— without asking for her resident's help. Next, she emailed the surgical team to thank them for their time and guidance and suggest a follow-up meeting to regroup that afternoon.

Here's what Veronica told me:

> It's a progression: you go from asking, "I'm going to do this—is that OK?" to saying, "I took care of it." Your supervisor is still with you,

FIGURE 8-4

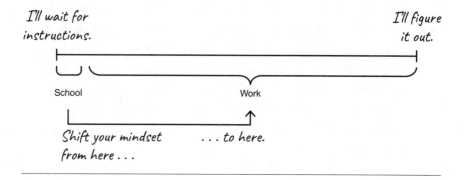

The mindset shift you'll need to make when you go from school to work

but your relationship with them changes. They are no longer your drill instructor telling you what to do. They become your coach, giving feedback and helping you grow. Ownership isn't about being independent. It's about taking responsibility. And taking responsibility includes knowing when you need to ask for help.

Veronica taught me a lesson: transitioning from school to work is about more than just making money and having a manager. It's about shifting from the mindset of *I'll wait for instructions* to the mindset of *I'll try to figure it out*. Figure 8-4 shows what this shift looks like.

But it's a journey. Everyone knows that it takes time to learn something new—anywhere from several days to several months, depending on the complexity of the role. When you first start a job, expectations of you will never be lower. But before long, you will "graduate"—and often without warning, as Veronica did. Different managers will have different working styles, of course. Some will graduate people faster than others. Some will appreciate your proactivity more than others. Some will respect your point of view more than others. But the responsibility will come—and people who once were waiting for you will now rely on your opinion and, above all, your *leadership*. The more comfortable you are with embracing such a mindset shift, the sooner people will be convinced of your competence—and the sooner you'll be able to make an impact.

Try This

- Before getting started on a new assignment, make sure you understand *what* you need to do, *how* you need to do it, and *by when* you need to do it.

- Bundle your questions, escalate them one level at a time, and show your homework with each person.

- Minimize others' workload when asking for help.

- If you see a problem or opportunity, be proactive about flagging (or even solving) it.

- Before asking your manager to review your work, ask yourself: Have I followed all directions I've been given? Have I focused on the details that matter? Do I have a call to action? Have I presented my work in a way that's easy for my manager to review? Have I prepared answers to questions my manager might ask? Have I figured out (and shared) what I plan to do next?

Manage Your Workload

In a typical workday you will be bombarded by an endless list of tasks. When you're new to the workforce, it's hard to know how to get everything done while not making mistakes *and* keeping everyone happy. It's hard enough just figuring out your assignments. First step: understand what tasks are urgent and important so you can prioritize correctly—and maintain your competence at every turn.

How to Define What's Urgent

Urgency is something we're all familiar with from school: the assignment with the nearest deadline is the most urgent; the assignment with the furthest deadline is the least urgent. This is true for the workplace as well, but urgency applies to more than just deadlines. In the workplace, urgency is defined by four factors (see figure 9-1).

- **Proximity.** How close you are to the deadline or, if you don't have a deadline, how long it's been since others started waiting. In general, the closer you are to the deadline or the longer people have been waiting for you, the more urgent the task is.

Know This

- You won't have enough hours in the day to do everything.

- To be competent while remaining sane, focus on what's important and urgent.

- **Scrutiny.** Who is involved in a project or initiative. In general, the more leverage (power) someone has over you, the more urgent it is to reply to them. So, the higher up someone is in your chain of command, the more urgent their requests should be considered, because they have the ability to shape your future in the organization. And the more you are relying on someone to do you a favor, the more urgent it is that you respond to them, because they can change their mind and decide not to help you anymore.

- **Anxiety.** How eager others are to move on. Recall the unspoken rule of *mirroring others*: the more urgently your colleagues are treating the situation, the more urgently they will likely expect you to treat it as well.

- **Time sensitivity.** Whether a task gets harder or your options get more limited as time passes, such as if you are trying to book time with someone. The longer you wait and the fewer options remain, the more urgent the task becomes. And if you have a task that needs to be done before other things can happen, that task is more urgent.

FIGURE 9-1

How to decide if something is urgent

$$\textit{Urgency} = \textit{proximity} \times \textit{scrutiny} \times \textit{anxiety} \times \textit{time sensitivity}$$

| How close you are to the deadline | Who is involved | How eager others are to move on | Whether things get harder over time |

FIGURE 9-2

How to decide if something is important

$$Importance = centrality \times scrutiny \times criticality$$

| How core the task is to your role | Who is affected or paying attention | How much the task matters to others |

How to Define What's Important

Importance is also something we're all familiar with from school: the assignments that count the most toward your final grade are the most important; the assignments that count the least are the least important. At work, though, the number of "points" you get from each assignment is unspoken, which means importance can be trickier to nail down. At work, importance is defined by three factors (see figure 9-2).

- **Centrality.** How core a certain task is to your role. Every task sits on a spectrum between have-to-do and nice-to-do. Since have-to-do tasks are what you were hired to do, the closer a task is to the have-to-do end of the spectrum, the more important it is for you to do it—and to do it well.

- **Scrutiny.** Who is affected or paying attention. The more a task affects people beyond you—and the more leverage those people have over you—the more important the task is.

- **Criticality.** How much something matters to others. If a certain task is critical to a project that the team or company cares about, then that task is considered important. One clue to uncover the criticality of a project is to observe the amount of attention it is getting from the higher-ups. If your boss's boss is asking for regular updates, the project is likely to be considered high-profile—and critical.

FIGURE 9-3

How to prioritize your work

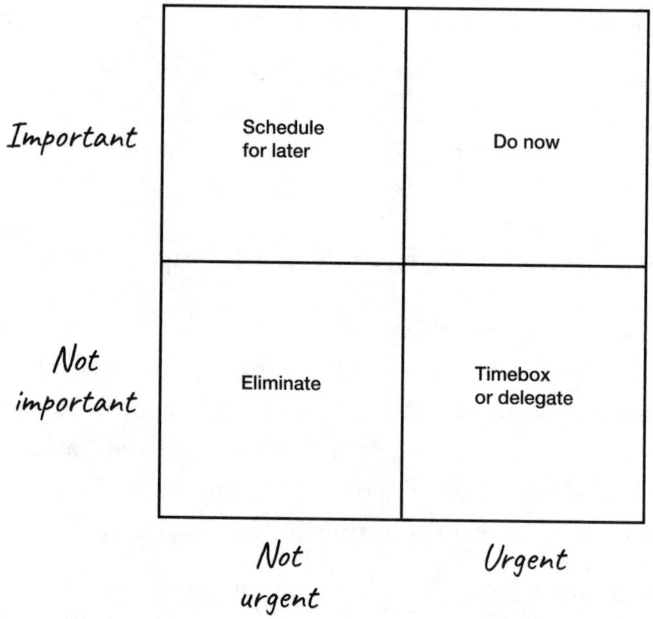

	Not urgent	Urgent
Important	Schedule for later	Do now
Not important	Eliminate	Timebox or delegate

How to Prioritize What's Urgent and Important

If we bring urgency and importance together, we get my adaptation of what's called the Eisenhower Matrix (see figure 9-3).[1]

If something is important and urgent, do it immediately.

If something is important but not urgent, schedule it for later.

If something is urgent but not important, "timebox" it—budget a certain amount of time to get it done, then go do it. Or, if you are a manager, delegate it to someone else.

If something is neither urgent nor important, remove it from your life.

If you have multiple tasks that all seem urgent and important, force yourself to rank your tasks from most important and urgent to least.

FIGURE 9-4

The tension between what you find important and what others find important

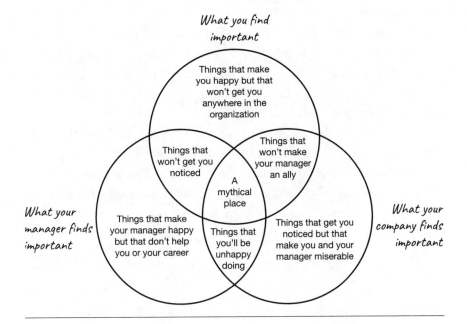

Of course, the framework considers what's important only from the perspective of other people (namely your manager). While this can be useful when you are new to the team and are trying to demonstrate your Three Cs, it isn't always sustainable or even desirable for your long-term career. What you find important may not be what your manager finds important. What your manager finds important may not be what your company finds important. What your company finds important may not be what you find important. Figure 9-4 shows the tension between what you find important and what others find important.

One area where what you care about can come into tension with what others care about is the domain of promotable tasks and nonpromotable tasks.[2] Promotable tasks are those that help you get ahead because the higher-ups care about them, whether it's building new features in a product or making the company money.[3] Nonpromotable tasks, also known as "office housework,"[4] are tasks like taking notes for other people, ordering lunch for a meeting, and organizing social events. These kinds of tasks might contribute to the greater good, but they don't necessarily help your career, unless these tasks are part of your job description.

The ability to distinguish between promotable and nonpromotable tasks can be especially important if you are a woman or a person of color. Studies have shown that engineers of color tend to receive less desirable assignments at work.[5] Women tend to both volunteer for and be asked to do office housework more often than men.[6] They also tend to be perceived more negatively when they say "no" to these tasks than a man does—and get less credit for saying "yes."[7]

How much you should worry about office housework depends on your context, of course. Receiving a task from a higher-up with leverage over you is different from being asked to do something by a coworker. Organizing team events when you are an administrative assistant is different from doing it when you are an engineer. Being asked to take notes when you are new—and still trying to prove your Three Cs—is different from being asked to take notes when you are no longer the most junior person on the team.

So, what do you do? Analyze the pros and cons: Do the benefits of volunteering outweigh the costs? Can you prove yourself, show your commitment, learn something new, meet more people, or help someone in need? What else could you do with the time? Step up if it makes sense. If not, let someone else volunteer. The opportunity may not be valuable for you, but it could be valuable for someone else. If you find yourself being assigned office housework constantly and need a way out, consider what a diversity and inclusion consultant suggested to me: ask your manager if the team can have a rotation system where everyone takes turns, say, taking notes in meetings. And stick to the schedule, even if other people don't. As a female insurance executive told me, "Lean on others. Don't do the work when it's their turn. If it doesn't get done, it's OK. Otherwise, some guys will just assume the girl will keep doing it if they slack. Don't let them." And if the work still somehow boomerangs back to you, try finding a more urgent and important assignment. That way, you can say, "I'd love to help, but I'm helping Brian with an important client workshop. This could be a great opportunity for Caleb or Rob, though, given their interest in _____. Have you asked them?" So, instead of framing your reply as "I don't want to do this" (which could make you sound uncommitted and incompatible), you can now frame your reply as "I want to help, but my circumstances don't allow me to." Push gently but firmly.

Even though we're discussing what *you* can do when faced with unfair amounts of office housework, know that the responsibility of distributing work more equitably shouldn't just fall on you. A more level playing field is everyone's responsibility—and that includes your manager and all of your teammates (and especially the men). It's not enough to expect women or people of color to say "no" more. Men need to step up and share the load.

How to Juggle Your Priorities

Although focusing on the most urgent and important priorities can help you tame an overwhelming set of tasks, doing so is rarely enough. You may reduce, say, ten tasks down to four, but still: if all four are both equally urgent and important, you still won't have enough time in the day to do everything—and do it all well. It's normal and expected to find yourself in such a situation. Let's walk through some strategies that I and others have found helpful.

Avoid surprises

Crystel, a field organizer on a political campaign, was in charge of almost everything. And everything felt both urgent and important: recruiting and managing volunteers, preparing and analyzing voter data, and sometimes even advising on policy.

While picking up her takeout dinner one evening, Crystel received a call from her boss, the campaign field director. Fifty volunteers were scheduled to knock on doors and needed a map of the homes to visit. Crystel had been preparing the maps all week and had also ordered a number of tablets to replace the usual printed copies. But her boss couldn't find the tablets.

Crystel checked her email and found a shipping update for her tablet order. The tablets had been delayed until the following evening. Her heart started racing. She had been so busy organizing the voter data that she'd forgotten to monitor the tablet shipment.

She explained the situation to her boss as she ran back to the campaign office. When she arrived, several of the volunteers had already shown up. Because Crystel and her colleagues had assumed everyone would be using tablets, no maps were printed. Over the following half hour, more volunteers arrived as Crystel and her boss scrambled to export the maps, find the clipboards, run to the local print shop to print the lists, and organize the volunteers. In the end, Crystel solved the problem—but kept fifty volunteers waiting around.

Crystel's challenge wasn't that the tablets didn't get delivered in time. It was that she didn't warn her boss as soon as possible and propose a plan to solve the problem before it impacted others. Imagine if Crystel had said this to her manager instead:

> *Hey, I just checked the tracking on the tablet order. The delivery has been delayed and so the order might not arrive until the day after the Thursday canvass. Three options: (1) I can try to order from another store that can deliver the tablets in time and then return the late shipment later, (2) I order locally and drive to pick them up, or (3) we revert to pen and paper on Thursday. All three are possible, but from what I've seen from the nearby electronics stores, option 2 might cost us $300 more in total. I think we have time to try option 1 first. What do you think?*

Had Crystel alerted her manager as soon as possible, her manager would have picked an option and both of them would have moved on. By letting her manager be surprised, Crystel let a constraint become a problem. It's about doing what you say you will do.

It all comes down to expectations—whether you exceed them or fall below them. Figure 9-5 shows how the difference between actual performance and expected performance can impact others' perceptions of you.

No one is superhuman. People understand that every situation has its trade-offs. When making promises to other managers or clients, your manager may say that work can be done cheaply, quickly, or with high quality. You may be able to achieve two of those, but rarely will you achieve all three. Your job is the same way. If your manager needs a one-day task done in one hour, you will need to make trade-offs. As long as you are being proactive, articulating the trade-offs, and giving reasonable explanations that frame your situation not as "I can't do this because I'm uncommitted" but as "I'm committed, but my hands are tied, so these are the options," people are generally understanding.

FIGURE 9-5

How to think about managing others' expectations

Your actual performance	>	Your expected performance	⟶ Impressed ☺
Your actual performance	=	Your expected performance	⟶ Satisfied ☺
Your actual performance	<	Your expected performance	⟶ Disappointed ☹

A warning: it helps to under-promise and over-deliver, but you need to be convincing with the signals you send. As we've discussed, everything you do and don't do sends a signal—and every signal contributes to others' impressions of how competent, committed, and compatible you may be. But your actions don't just send signals. Over time, your signals become *patterns of behavior*. Once people can explain your behavior using the phrase "Whenever . . . always . . . ," you've established a pattern (for example, "*Whenever* a patient needs help, Saba *always* has an excuse to step away" was a pattern of behavior I heard about from a youth counselor at a hospital). Establish a pattern of being the one who never surprises your teammates. Surprises may be fun on a birthday, but they aren't much fun when it comes to broken promises and missed deadlines.

Stay ahead of patterns

In elementary school we learned that if we see three circles followed by a square, and then another three circles, what should follow next is another square. This is the ability to recognize patterns. Pattern recognition isn't just something from kindergarten. It is a life skill that can help you not only do better work but better manage work—and your life.

Let's look at some tactics.

How to Manage Others' Expectations

Can you see a surprise ahead? Here's what to say to manage expectations.

If you don't think you can commit to something, try saying, "I'm happy to help, but I have _____ that will conflict with _____ because _____. Would _____ work?"

If you might be late to something, try saying, "In my calendar I have _____ right before _____, so I might be about _____ minutes late. Would that be OK?"

If you can't meet a deadline, try saying, "Unfortunately, with _____ and _____ I suspect I might only finish _____ by _____. Would it be possible to _____?"

If you aren't sure you can meet an expectation, try saying, "Given _____, I can do _____ by _____ time or I can do _____ by _____ time. Which do you prefer?"

If your plans have changed, try saying, "Just a heads-up that _____, which might impact _____ and might require _____. I'll keep you posted, but wanted to let you know."

IDENTIFY PROBLEMS AT THEIR ROOT CAUSE. When you confront a problem, don't just solve it once, only to have to solve a similar flavor of the same problem again later. Figure out *why* the problem happened in the first place so that you can prevent it from causing trouble again.

Isaiah, a farm manager, was doing his daily walk down a row of tomato crops when he noticed something: some leaves on one of the tomato plants were turning yellow. It had been a dry growing season, so Isaiah watered the yellow patch and then got busy with his other duties and forgot about it. Several days later, Isaiah noticed that a few more plants had started turning yellow. Isaiah once again pulled out the hose and started watering. A week later, Isaiah's boss showed up to inspect the farm. She noticed the yellow patches immediately.

"Isaiah, why are these tomato leaves yellow?"

"I'm not sure."

"Have you been watering them?"

"Yes."

"Did you apply the NPK fertilizer?"

"Yes."

"Have you tested the nutrients?"

"No."

"Have you tested the pH?"

"No."

"Have you looked for pests?"

"No."

"Have you isolated any of the affected plants?"

"No."

"Have you spoken with nearby farmers to see if they've faced a similar issue?"

"No."

"When did you notice this problem?"

"A week ago."

"Isaiah! What are you waiting for?!"

Isaiah explained that he had been busy fixing the tractor, directing the farmhands, and calling the irrigation company. He added that he'd wanted to see how the yellow patch would progress. His boss was not impressed. She told me:

> Discoloration could be due to a dozen problems, anything from a minor watering problem to a serious infection. The crop life cycle is only about six weeks, so a week is a long time to not be doing anything. You have to separate the affected crops immediately before the problem spreads to the entire farm. You can't just say "I don't know" and wait. You have to take control of the situation.

Many other managers have told me something similar: if you see a negative pattern, whether it's a repeating error message, several customer complaints, or a regular equipment malfunction, it's important to not simply monitor or patch up the problem, but to *fix* the underlying cause. Otherwise, the negative pattern could return—and you'll waste valuable time chasing yet another symptom. If you see a problem happening twice, don't let it happen a third time. To identify the root cause, ask "Why is this happening?" Then, keep asking "Why?" until you uncover the underlying cause. Once you have a hypothesis of what's going on, report back to your manager with what you've learned. For example:

Hi _____,

I looked into _____ and suspect what's happening is _____. Would it be appropriate for me to _____?
I suggest this because _____.

Thanks,

_____

Then, keep investigating the problem until you not only find the root cause but also have a few solutions to offer your manager. For example:

Hi _____,

I wanted to give you an update on _____. I investigated and found that _____. The options are to _____ or _____. Given _____, my suggestion is to _____, but I wanted to run it by you. Would that option make sense? I'll go with it if I don't hear from you by _____. [You can include a deadline if your boss doesn't always reply quickly and you've earned enough leeway to pull this off.]

Best,

_____

When you're new, you may not have the background knowledge to uncover the root cause on your own. That's fine. And when you are working in a team, you may not be able to address the root cause on your own, either. That's fine, too. The important thing is to be in control of the problem as much as you can—and that begins with understanding what's really going on.

PREEMPT PATTERNS. The habits of the people you work with are more than just habits; they are patterns—and hidden opportunities for you to take control of the situation before the situation takes control of you. If your boss's boss has a habit of creating fire drills (sudden urgent and important requests that require your undivided attention) the day after holidays, consider clearing your schedule after the next holiday to accommodate the likely flare-up. If your manager has a habit of asking for project progress updates each Friday, consider offering them an update before the next Friday. If a coworker has a habit of responding to emails between 7 and 8 a.m., consider timing your next email so it reaches their inbox when they are most likely to reply.

The strategy of staying one step ahead can apply to more than just your boss. A freelance project manager told me about how, whenever multiple clients asked for something similar (for example, a certain design project management workplan), he'd create a template that he could easily customize. This works for emails, too. If you find yourself sending the same kinds of messages over and over, make it as easy as hitting Copy and Paste. Doing so can help you free up time for more important and urgent matters, rather than have to start each task from scratch.

Get your point across

When you are working on a team, you won't always have full control over how you tackle an urgent and important task. You need to communicate with—and rely upon—other people. But there's a problem: just because you communicate doesn't mean you get your point across. To maximize your chances of getting your message across and, ultimately, getting what you need, it helps to keep in mind the following assumptions:

- People don't know what you know.

- People haven't read what you sent.

- People aren't fully paying attention when you're speaking.

- People don't remember what you said or what they agreed to.

- People don't have the time or attention span you have.

Protect What's Sacred

Achieving harmony between work and life isn't easy—especially when you are juggling multiple priorities or working from home.

Bobby, a sales rep I interviewed, told me how easy it was for him to drift in his personal routine when he started working from home while also balancing a startup on the side. First, he abandoned his usual morning run to make more time for answering email. Next, he started working later into the night to clear his inbox for the following day. Then, he replaced his home-cooked meals with pizza, soda, and beer. Before long, he felt like garbage.

Bobby's partner, an avid follower of mindfulness, encouraged him to start meditating and engaging in breathing exercises. Several weeks later, Bobby began to see a therapist. A few weeks after that, he replaced his pizza with vegetables, started drinking more water, and began working out again. Bobby eventually returned to his prior self; only this time, he established new, more productive patterns like scheduling tasks around when he had the most energy, logging off at 5:30 p.m. every day, and following a consistent sleep schedule. Bobby realized that *whenever* he ate and slept poorly, he *always* felt bad; *whenever* he slept and exercised well, he *always* worked well. It didn't take long to see what patterns worked—and didn't work—for his mind and body. It all came down to recognizing patterns—and protecting what's sacred: what Bobby called his emotional immune system.

Nisha, a university administrator and mother of a young child, established her patterns even before she started her job:

> Being a mom is important to me, so I told my manager that my family comes first. I had to be up-front that if the university was going to have me, it would have to have my entire family—and if me working from home on Fridays, and coming in early and leaving early, didn't work, then this job wouldn't work. When

I showed up, I reminded people so there were no surprises. I made it clear that I'm still delivering—just on a different schedule.

Nisha taught me another lesson: you don't have go it alone. Every time she switched managers, departments, or jobs, Nisha immediately looked for coworkers who were in situations similar to hers who could become allies in protecting what was sacred. Often, all it took was a question like, "Hey, did I overhear that you're also juggling both work and _____? I'd love your advice on how you made it work." Before long, she had strength in numbers.

Don't worry if you can't find allies and haven't set expectations up-front. It's not too late. Consider what a diversity, inclusion, and belonging leader told me and wait until you've received two solid pieces of positive feedback from your manager. Then, approach your manager, explain the factors that are outside of your control, share what you've already done to solve the problem yourself, and express how willing you are to match others' commitment—but on your own terms:

> By the way, I was hoping to get your advice on a challenge I've been facing. I didn't appreciate how crazy traffic can get, so the difference between leaving at 4:30 p.m. and 5:00 p.m. is the difference between being stuck in traffic for one hour and two. I've tried taking other routes and carpooling. I'd love to discuss an arrangement that would allow me to leave at 4:30 p.m. while still making sure I'm delivering. Can I come in early or log back in later in the evening?

Luckily, more organizations than ever are realizing that what matters isn't your *input* (how hard it looks like you're working), but rather your *output* (what you accomplish). If your company is stuck in the past, you may need to push gently and firmly to get what you need.

So, what can you do? Try the following strategies:

- If you are making a point, start with the background information, using an opening phrase like, "The background is . . . ," "The context is . . . ," or "The goal is . . ."

- If you are sharing something complicated, start with your main point and limit yourself to three supporting points.

- If you are sharing emails or documents, make your message as short as possible.

- If you are making multiple points or talking for a long time, pause occasionally and let others comment or ask questions before moving on.

Beyond *what* you say, *how* you say it can be just as important. Table 9-1 offers a few options for getting your message across.

So You Made a Mistake. Now What?

We all make mistakes; it's how we learn and grow. If you aren't making mistakes, you may not be stretching yourself enough. And in the workplace, what you need to worry about usually isn't making a mistake per se; it's the *kind* of mistake you make. Figure 9-6 lists several types of mistakes and shows how they compare.

Some mistakes are worse than others, of course. But unless you accidentally project a cat video onto your CEO's investor presentation, try not to worry too much—your coworkers have likely seen worse. The reality is this: Some mistakes are simply irreversible—there is nothing you can do to change the situation, no matter how bad it is. All you can do is apologize, explain what happened, and share how you will avoid making the mistake again. Showing your competence and commitment isn't about never making mistakes. It's about owning up, gracefully recovering, and not making the same mistake twice. Figure 9-7 has suggestions for how to respond to different kinds of mistakes.

TABLE 9-1

How to communicate effectively so you get what you want

If you have . . .	Try to . . .
Lots of data or details to compare	Create a chart, graph, or table
An idea that's hard to imagine	Share a picture, sketch, mock-up, or example
An edited version of a document	Track your changes and add comments explaining your thought process
Specific details from a prior document you want to reference	Send a screenshot or the original file with the relevant sections highlighted
Information from a specific source that others might want to reference	Share a hyperlink to the web page
A file with formatting that could show up differently on different devices	Save and send your file as a PDF
A file where people need to manipulate the information	Save and send a raw editable file
A decision you want to document to avoid any misunderstandings	Send an email documenting the decision
Lots of details for people to sift through, think about, or comment on	Send a file for people to review on their own time (plus schedule a follow-up meeting if needed)
A topic that's complicated, controversial, or requires discussion	Schedule a call or meeting
A meeting to schedule	Send a calendar invitation with the date, time, and meeting method clearly stated
A decision that requires multiple people's approval	Consult people individually, then bring the idea to the entire group

FIGURE 9-6

Different types of mistakes

No mistakes	are better than	mistakes.
Safe mistakes	are better than	dangerous mistakes.
Small mistakes	are better than	big mistakes.
Private mistakes	are better than	public mistakes.
First-time mistakes	are better than	non-first-time mistakes.

FIGURE 9-7

How to respond to different kinds of mistakes

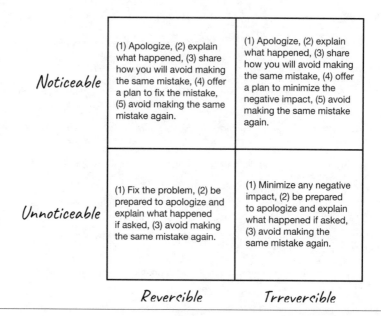

	Reversible	Irreversible
Noticeable	(1) Apologize, (2) explain what happened, (3) share how you will avoid making the same mistake, (4) offer a plan to fix the mistake, (5) avoid making the same mistake again.	(1) Apologize, (2) explain what happened, (3) share how you will avoid making the same mistake, (4) offer a plan to minimize the negative impact, (5) avoid making the same mistake again.
Unnoticeable	(1) Fix the problem, (2) be prepared to apologize and explain what happened if asked, (3) avoid making the same mistake again.	(1) Minimize any negative impact, (2) be prepared to apologize and explain what happened if asked, (3) avoid making the same mistake again.

As much as we frame this chapter as a set of mindsets and strategies for what you can do as an individual to manage your workload, it's important to keep in mind that not everything is within your control. It may be your job to take ownership over your sanity, but it's the job of your manager (and their manager) to create work conditions where you can remain sane.

In business, people often like to say that culture is set from the top. It's true. If company leaders have a pattern of creating fire drills, it can be difficult for their subordinates (and *their* subordinates) to push back. And once this culture trickles down, layer by layer, to those who have the least leverage, you end up with the attitude of "Well, that's just how things have always been done."

While this may be discouraging in the short run (especially if you find yourself in such an environment), I hope that it can be empowering in the long run. The person in charge may be someone else today, but before long it will be you. And when that time comes, it will be your responsibility to make sure your team stays sane. Remember what worked—and didn't work—for you. If everything worked well for you, learn from those for whom things didn't work so well. The culture will be yours to build. Create one that you will be proud of!

Try This

- Prioritize what's urgent and important. Before starting a task, consider how urgent and important it is compared to everything else you have to do.

- Avoid surprises. Manage others' expectations by being up-front and proactive about what you can deliver and what you can't, given the constraints you are under.

- Get your point across. Be deliberate about when and how you communicate so that you maximize the chance that others receive and understand your message.

- Stay ahead of patterns. Recognize repeating elements in the people and situations around you, then figure out how you can make these patterns work for—and not against—you.

GETTING ALONG
WITH EVERYONE

10

Read between the People

W hat are you doing? Leave that alone!" snapped Sue, the head of the department.

Alison froze. She had been using her break to clean the supply closet when Sue appeared in the doorway. "Um, OK . . ." she stammered. *I was only going to throw out those empty cartons*, she thought after Sue stormed off. *What's the big deal?*

The next morning, Sue appeared again while Alison was talking to her manager, Michael. "You shouldn't have done that," she growled.

Alison was confused. "I'm sorry. What?" She looked at Michael, who was silent.

"Did you not have work? Why were you cleaning the closet?"

"Um, I was just looking for something and saw it was messy, so I decided to clean it."

"That's my job. Not yours."

"I'm sorry," Alison said. "I'll make sure to ask first next time."

"Yes. Do that."

Once Sue was gone, Michael motioned to a nearby meeting room. "Let's chat," he whispered to Alison. They walked in and closed the door.

"What's this all about?" Michael asked.

Know This

- The most important people aren't always at the top.

- The better you can learn the hidden relationships between and the invisible boundaries surrounding your coworkers, the more compatible you will be (and the more effective you will be at getting things done).

"I'm not sure," Alison said. "I was cleaning the supply closet, then Sue showed up and told me to stop."

"Ah. Yeah, the closet has been a disaster for years. But Sue keeps a lot of her stuff in there. One time, someone threw out a bunch of her stuff without telling her. She's been paranoid about the closet ever since."

What happened? Alison overlooked the hidden relationships and invisible boundaries of her team. As a result, she unintentionally overshot her zone of commitment—and became threatening and incompatible to Sue. When we look at any organization from the outside, all we see is a collection of people. But that tells only part of the story. It's the hidden relationships between people and the invisible boundaries surrounding them that are really fascinating—and that are important to decipher when you are new. To avoid ending up in Alison's situation, and to maximize your compatibility, take the time to identify the hidden relationships in your organization.

Identify the Chain of Command

Learning the chain of command—who reports to whom—is one of the most important things you can do when you are new to a team. Your primary tool will be an org chart, a diagram showing each person in the organization and their reporting lines. If you work at a large organization, this will be in your team's shared folder or online portal. Solid lines show who someone's direct manager is (or who is a subordinate to whom), while dotted lines show who someone's secondary manager is.

FIGURE 10-1

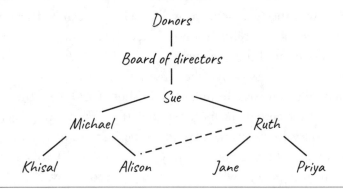

The visible (and invisible) chain of command

Not everyone will have a secondary manager, but if you do, you will face one of two setups: either your primary and secondary managers will jointly evaluate your performance (in which case it's important to keep both happy) or only your primary manager will evaluate you (in which case keeping your primary manager happy is your main objective). Figure 10-1 shows how Alison's company is organized.

If your organization doesn't have an org chart, there are other ways to figure out who reports to whom.

Pay attention to how people speak

If you hear that Alison "reports to" Michael or is Michael's "direct report," that means Michael is Alison's boss. You might also hear that "Sue is Alison's 'skip manager,'" which means Sue is the boss of Alison's boss. If you hear others describe projects as "cross-functional" or "cross-departmental," that means teams frequently work with people in other departments—so you might want to figure out who's who in those departments as well.

Pay attention to how people behave

Does Michael's behavior change when Sue joins the call or enters the room? Does Michael pause all conversation and direct attention to Sue?

Everyone stands or sits a little straighter when their boss is in the room. Some manager-subordinate relationships are friendlier than others, so how someone behaves when their manager is present can tell you a lot about how well they get along (as well as who you can be friendly with and who to be more careful around). Look also at when meetings start: typically, it's not until the boss shows up.

Everyone has a boss—even the bosses. You just might not see them. Ultimately, whoever pays the bills calls the shots. CEOs have their boards of directors. Even entrepreneurs have bosses. If you're an entrepreneur who received money from investors, your "bosses" are your investors. Or if you run a nonprofit, your bosses are your donors. You have a boss even if you're an entrepreneur who funded your own company. Your "bosses" are your clients and customers.

Deciphering the chain of command is valuable because you understand not only how everyone contributes to the overall mission of the team but also who has leverage over whom. This knowledge can help you avoid overshooting the zone of commitment and coming across as threatening, as Alison did. Overshooting tends to happen in three ways: going to someone's manager with a problem without first trying to resolve the problem with the person one-on-one, making someone look bad in front of their boss, or failing to acknowledge the invisible hierarchy when people of different ranks are together. Next time you receive an email, look at the order of the names at the top. If an email is addressed to a senior vice president named Michele, a vice president named Hasib, and an analyst named Eugenio, people will often write "Hi Michele, Hasib, and Eugenio" as a subtle nod to everyone's roles. If the hierarchy isn't obvious, people might list recipients alphabetically or simply write "Hi all."

Identify the Influencers

Once you've identified the formal powers on your new team, the next step is to identify the *informal* powers—the influencers. These are the people who may not have the authority to make decisions, but do have the leverage to influence decisions. Influencers come in five types (with some people occupying more than one role).

Gatekeepers. People (often they're assistants) who work closely with the senior leaders—and who can influence whether you get to meet with them and how they perceive you.

Veterans. People who've worked in the organization the longest—and who can help you learn how to effectively navigate the system based on what has and hasn't worked before.

Experts. People whom others tend to listen to or who know a particular topic well—and can help make you make your ideas more palatable to others.

Socialites. People who are known and respected around the organization—and who can introduce you to the right people and shape others' perceptions of you.

Advisers. People whom your manager and other senior people tend to trust—even if it's not clear why—and who can help you convince the higher-ups to agree with your ideas.

Of course, no one walks around with these labels on their foreheads. You need to observe your coworkers' behavior and recognize patterns. Do meetings or decisions always have to go through a particular person? You may have found a gatekeeper. Is someone always invited to meetings, asked for their opinion, or brought up as someone you should talk to? You may have found a veteran, expert, or socialite. Does your manager always reference the opinion of a particular colleague? You may have found an adviser. Once you've found an influencer, introduce yourself to them. Get to know them. And though it's important to be nice to everyone, be especially gracious with them.

I learned this last lesson from Rebecca, the head of a research lab. Rebecca had an executive assistant named Christian. Christian wasn't high up in the chain of command and didn't have any formal decision-making power. But what Christian did have was Rebecca's trust. In fact, Rebecca trusted Christian so much that she'd regularly ask for his opinion on whether to hire someone. One time, a job candidate stormed through the door and—without a "Good morning," or "Please"—declared, "I need to talk to Rebecca." After asking the person to have a seat, Christian messaged Rebecca:

> The candidate is here for her interview. She's rude.

And just like that, the interview ended before it even began—all because Christian, Rebecca's gatekeeper, decided to keep the gate shut.

Influencers don't have to be door closers, though. They can be door openers, as I learned from Amira, a sales representative for a technology company. Amira was about to secure a large client, but the client wanted an unusually large discount for the first year of the software license. Amira tried convincing her manager that the one-year discount would be worthwhile long term, but her manager disagreed. Refusing to take "no" for an answer, Amira contacted Jarron, a mentor of hers who also happened to be someone her manager listened to. In his next conversation with Amira's manager, Jarron casually mentioned how effective discounts could be for driving sales, without ever mentioning Amira or her situation. Amira's idea got approved that afternoon.

While influencers may seem like a relic of large corporations, they exist everywhere—even at startups. In fact, sometimes the organizations that claim to be "flat"—with everyone at the same level and no one leading—are the most hierarchical. It's natural: the harder it is to figure out who does what based on job titles, the more it seems like everyone is in charge, but no one is in charge—and the more people need to rely on their informal authority to get things done. The startup's leadership may have simply erased the lines in the chain of command but kept the structure. Be alert!

Identify the Swimlanes

Once you've identified the people, you may want to identify each person's swimlane, or what they are responsible for and when. If you ever hear someone say "So-and-so needs to stay in their lane," they're really saying "So-and-so needs to stop trying to do my job." Swimlanes are not to be confused with job titles.

The culture of your team matters when it comes to swimlanes. In general, workplace cultures sit somewhere along the spectrum between "ask for permission" and "beg for forgiveness." (Table 10-1 shows the two

TABLE 10-1

Norms to look out for when deciphering a new team culture

"Ask for permission" culture	"Beg for forgiveness" culture
Everyone has their own specific responsibilities.	Everyone does a bit of everything.
People seem to care more about who's the boss.	People seem to care more about who has the best ideas.
People seem to care more about doing things the "right"/safe way.	People seem to care more about doing things the "innovative"/quick way.

extremes.) If everyone on your team sticks to their own job duties, listens to the person with the highest title over the one with the best ideas, and values doing things the "right" or safe way, then you're likely dealing with a team that leans closer to the "ask for permission" end of the spectrum. In that case, consider getting into the habit of asking your manager, "Is there anyone I should speak with before moving forward?" to avoid overstepping.

If everyone on your team does a bit of everything, prioritizes good ideas over job titles, and values doing things the "innovative" or quick way, then you're likely dealing with a team that leans closer to the "beg for forgiveness" end of the spectrum. In that case, you'll need to get comfortable saying, "I wanted to let you know that I did _____," because your swimlane isn't rigidly bound.

When in doubt, ask for permission. Asking for permission is especially important when you are working remotely, since often you can't tell who is working on what until you've overstepped. One time, a finance intern was asked to update a big spreadsheet that was to be used by multiple teams. He updated the document, then shared it with the other teams himself, not realizing his manager had to approve it first. The manager got in trouble for not keeping an eye on him. The intern didn't receive a full-time job offer. The lesson? Even if your team has a "beg for forgiveness" culture, you're often better off asking for permission—and keeping your manager CC'd in your emails outside of the team—at least until your manager tells you to stop bothering them (which you should consider a compliment toward your competence).

Identify the Loyalties

As much as we'd like to think we're all in it together at work, people have their loyalties. One former high school teacher I interviewed told me about a time when she transferred to a new school. When she arrived, she kept hearing her coworkers complain about the school principal. She didn't get along with the principal either, so one day she criticized him in front of one of the vice principals. *This vice principal is on my side*, she thought. *After all, she's so nice to me.* Little did the teacher know that the vice principal was good friends with the principal—and ended up telling him what she said. This teacher called what she learned *the lesson of first loyalties*: though people may be friendly (and even loyal) to you, their *first* loyalty may be to someone else.

Remote work can make loyalties difficult to identify, but doing it is important nevertheless. Look for the cliques. Is José always talking about Kweku and James? Is Kweku always replying to James's group messages? Do José, Kweku, and James always show up together, or not at all, to remote socials? If so, you may have identified a clique; be aware that what you share with James will probably make its way over to José and Kweku.

While it's generally a good idea to avoid gossip and be thoughtful about who you associate with, don't let the fear of politics deter you from being social. This section isn't meant to paralyze you; it's meant to empower you to strategically navigate your new environment. Now, you know who to go to (and not go to) and who might be an ally (and not an ally). Consider it a tool in your tool kit for protecting yourself and getting what you want.

Identify the Comfort Zones

Once you are familiar with the people and the hidden relationships between them, the final step is to understand the comfort zones—the behaviors, jokes, language, and conversation topics that your team finds appropriate and inappropriate. Although every team is different, there are certain subjects that tend to be taboo. Table 10-2 points out a few topics to avoid and suggests what to talk about instead.

You may also find that people have different comfort zones around how openly and directly people communicate. An HR manager at a cosmetics

TABLE 10-2

Conversation topics to try—and avoid—at work

Instead of these topics . . .	. . . try these topics
Dating life	Academic background
Partying and drinking	Interests outside of work
Coworker gossip	Prior travels or future travel plans
Salary or income	Prior work experiences
Religion	Current projects
Politics	Pets and kids
Family or relationship issues	Weekend plans

company told me, "I work in a very emotional company. Anything that can be seen as remotely aggressive is off limits. Even saying 'no' can be a turnoff here. Instead of saying 'no,' people around here say, 'Hmm, interesting. What about this other option?'"

Since even the people I interviewed had a hard time explaining their team's comfort zones, the key is to recognize patterns and mirror others. When was the last time someone on your team said something, only for everyone in the room to pause awkwardly and then switch topics? How much do people share about their weekends? What's the worst curse word or crudest joke you've heard anyone crack publicly? Learn the limits and stay within them.

Just as there's often a deeper meaning behind what's explicitly stated in a text, there are hidden relationships behind the interactions that take place at work. Often, it's not the brilliance of your ideas that determines how impactful you are; instead, it's about how you navigate relationships. The earlier you make sense of the people around you, the more effectively you'll be able to work the system—and the more impact you'll have. Start observing.

Try This

- Identify the chain of command: figure out who reports to whom and, when in doubt, respect the invisible hierarchy.

- Identify the influencers: be on the lookout for—and build relationships with—gatekeepers, veterans, experts, socialites, and advisers.

- Identify the swimlanes: figure out who is in charge of what and, when in doubt, ask for permission before starting new tasks or sharing work outside of your team.

- Identify the first loyalties: uncover who is loyal to whom and what the cliques are.

- Identify the comfort zones: figure out the behaviors, jokes, language, and conversation topics your team finds acceptable and unacceptable—and try to stay within those limits.

Spark Relationships

Y ou may have heard the saying "It's not *what* you know but *who* you know." It's true. People make hiring and firing decisions, people decide who should receive career-building assignments, and people decide who will be invited to important meetings.

At one accounting firm, for example, the senior managers met at the end of each year to rate the junior employees. If a certain manager had worked with you, they'd give you a rating (hopefully a high one). If a manager had interacted with you at a company social event, they'd also rate you. A small percentage of employees would be rated "above expectations"—meaning they would be on the fast track for promotion and would receive a larger bonus.

The same pattern emerged year after year: the employees who received the largest bonuses and fastest promotions weren't always the hardest or most competent workers; they were the ones who had the most managers praising them behind closed doors. The employees who were rated "below expectations" didn't necessarily have the lowest competence; they were the people that no one knew.

Success isn't just about getting ahead, of course. It's also about having a support network you can rely on and confide in when life gets tough. Building relationships with colleagues is an important part of enjoying your job. Work would be a miserable place if the only thing people did was stare at their computer screens all day.

Know This

- The first time you do anything is always uncomfortable. The second time is always easier.

- Building professional relationships comes down to finding excuses to spark that first interaction, then finding small ways to sustain the momentum.

And if you happen to be just out of school, you may soon find yourself having the same complaint as every other recent grad I've met: it can be really, really, really hard to meet people in the real world. So why not start with the people you work with?

If that sentence gives you the sweats, I get it. As an introvert—and a self-conscious one at that—I know how hard this can be. You might be thinking, *People don't want to talk to me. I have nothing interesting to say. I have nothing in common with them.* But whatever you may be feeling, I have likely felt it too. And while I'd like to say that I have overcome this anxiety, I haven't. My heart pounds every time I enter a room of strangers—and keeps pounding long after I leave. A million thoughts flood into my head: *Should I not have said that? Where did that awkward pause come from? Why did they raise their eyebrows when I said _____?*

To build relationships and overcome the anxiety that comes with it, I have found it helpful to break things down into three steps: spark the connection, play the game, and sustain the momentum.

Spark the Connection

Imagine you are walking by a tennis court with your racket. Suddenly, someone calls out to you. They've got a ball in one hand and a racket in the other. "Wanna play?" they ask. You've just found a tennis partner.

Now, replace the tennis court with the hallway of your workplace or the work instant messaging tool. Replace the "Wanna play?" with a nod, a smile, or a "How are things going?" or "Any plans for the weekend?" The setting and gestures may be different, but the idea is the same.

According to marriage expert Dr. John Gottman, these subtle gestures mean something. They're "bids"—requests for human connection.[1] Picking up on, and responding positively to, others' bids is important. In fact, according to Dr. Gottman, couples who stay married tend to be better at noticing and responding positively to their partner's bids. Couples who divorce tend to miss or reject their partner's bids. Strengthening relationships is about acknowledging others' presence and showing that you care. Saying "thank you" when someone opens the door for you or responding to an IM is sometimes all it takes.

Now we'll discuss how to spark connections, whether you're making the first move or just engaging with the people around you.

How to make the first move

You don't have to wait for others to reach out to you—you can reach out first. You have several groups of people at your fingertips. Let's walk through your options.

FOR PEOPLE YOU KNOW OR WORK NEAR. Try to find an excuse to spark a conversation. Whether you're working in person or remotely, use the few minutes before meetings start to talk to whoever arrived early. The topic doesn't have to be significant. Whether it's the weather ("Wow, it's freezing outside!"), an observation about work ("We've got quite the agenda for this meeting!"), or even the day of the week ("Happy Friday!"), the idea is simply to turn silence into dialogue. Once you and the other person have acknowledged each other, ask a question like, "How is your week so far?" or "Whereabouts are you calling from?" or "I'm a fan of your video chat background! Where was that photo taken?"

Similarly, the time when people are waiting for something can be a chance to spark conversation. When you are waiting for the elevator or standing in the lunch line, take the chance to talk to someone. If you are traveling for work, consider asking if anyone wants to share a ride.

After meetings, presentations, or life events, consider reaching out to a coworker and asking, "How do you think that meeting went?" "How did the presentation go?" or "How was the wedding?" People appreciate you caring, remembering, and, above all, listening.

FOR PEOPLE YOU DON'T KNOW BUT COULD BE INTRODUCED TO.
Consider asking for an introduction from someone you know. When requesting an introduction, show your homework, get to the point, and include a clear call to action. Here's an example.

Hi Nanako,

Nice to see you the other day! How did your presentation go?

I am wondering if you might be close enough to Triston Francis to make an introduction. I'm working on a research project on _____ and noticed that he worked at _____ and you are connected to him on LinkedIn. I was hoping to get his perspective on _____. If you would be open to making an intro, let me know if it'd help for me to send you a blurb about myself to pass along.

If I caught you at a bad time, no pressure at all—let me know either way.

Best,

Shuo

The etiquette is generally as follows: First, your contact forwards your introduction to the person you want to meet. If that person agrees to meet you, your contact will email both of you with a personal blurb introducing both sides.

Shuo: Please meet Triston Francis, a mentor and current _____.

Triston: Please meet Shuo Chen, a colleague and current _____ who is interested in speaking with you about _____.

Hope you all get a chance to connect!

Best,

Nanako

Then you or the other person will reply and move your contact to BCC to acknowledge that the connection has been made and to save the mutual connection from being flooded with scheduling emails.

Nanako: Thanks so much for the intro. Moving you to BCC.

Triston: Nice to e-meet you. Appreciate your willingness to connect. Might you be open to a phone or video call in the coming days? My availability is as follows (all times PT):

- Tue 10/27: before 2 p.m., after 3 p.m.

- Wed 10/28: anytime

- Thu 10/29: before 2 p.m., 3–4 p.m.

- Fri 10/30: anytime

If the above times do not work, please feel free to suggest alternatives that work for you.

Looking forward to chatting,

Shuo

Once the two sides find a mutually convenient time and medium to meet, one side (often the person requesting the meeting) sends a calendar invitation:

To: Triston Francis

Subject: Triston-Shuo call re: nonprofit experience

Location: Shuo to call Triston at 617-123-4567

Time: Wed 10/28, 2–3 p.m.

After talking, the person who requested the meeting sends an email to thank the other person for their time. It is also common for them to become connections on LinkedIn.

Hi Triston,

Thanks so much for taking time out of your busy schedule to chat earlier. It was great hearing about your experiences with _____. I especially appreciate your advice about _____ and will be sure to _____. Thanks also for your willingness to introduce me to your colleague, _____. Here is a brief introduction to help you out:

Shuo Chen is a _____ who is currently working on _____ and is interested in speaking with you about _____.

Looking forward to staying in touch,

Shuo

This type of interaction might feel transactional, but it happens all the time in the professional world. It's called the "double opt-in intro" (meaning both sides opt in to being introduced). This is how many people get jobs or even new clients—by asking for an introduction to a "second-degree connection," meeting them over the phone or video chat, adding them on LinkedIn, and then asking for a referral or another introduction. This is why it's so important to build relationships—because the more people you know directly, the more people you can access *indirectly*. It's not only about who *you* know but also about who *they* know.

FOR PEOPLE YOU DON'T KNOW AND CAN'T BE INTRODUCED TO. Consider sending a cold email. Here's an example.

Hi _____,

My name is _____ and I am a fellow _____. Hope you are doing well.

I am currently looking to transition from _____ to _____ and came across your profile on _____, which spoke to me because, like you, I also _____.

I was wondering if you might have a few minutes in the coming days/weeks to share your experience with me over the phone? My availability is as follows (all times PT):

- Tue 10/27: before 2 p.m., after 3 p.m.

- Wed 10/28: anytime

- Thu 10/29: before 2 p.m., 3–4 p.m.

- Fri 10/30: anytime

No worries if I caught you at a bad time—let me know either way.

Looking forward to hearing from you,

_____

Again, contacting strangers can feel awkward and needy at first, but people do it all the time. Most just do it poorly by not knowing their audience and failing to fully customize their email. This is what all the blanks in the examples are for. People like people who are like them, so the more you can present yourself as a younger version of the other person, with a reason to get in touch with them specifically, the more likely they are to reply. A good test is to ask yourself, *Would my email still make sense if I sent it to the wrong person?* If the answer is yes, your email isn't customized enough—and your recipient will likely ignore you out of a suspicion that you spammed a dozen other people with the same message. Reread your email and make sure that every possible detail is customized to the recipient, and that the message is short, organized, and easy to skim. Make it easy for people to help you!

How to be present and seen

Giving and receiving bids is not a solo activity. You need to be around other people. Here are some ideas for increasing your proximity to others, both physically and virtually.

IF YOU ARE WORKING ON-SITE, TRY TO STAY CLOSE TO YOUR TEAM.
You may not have any say in where your desk is located, but if it's far
away from your team members', consider asking your manager or HR
if you can be stationed closer to improve your productivity. If that isn't
possible, try passing by people's desks when you're walking around your
workplace and saying hello. Consider proposing social plans like, "I'll be
grabbing lunch at noon. Anyone want to join?" so you aren't relying on
others to remember to invite you. Or, consider making impromptu announcements over group chat like, "I'm grabbing coffee. Anyone want
anything or want to tag along?"

**IF YOU ARE REMOTE WHILE OTHERS ARE ON-SITE, BE SEEN—NOT
JUST HEARD.** Consider befriending at least one person who is working
on-site. That way, you are aware of what's going on and have someone to
advocate for you even when you aren't in the room. You could also suggest
using video chats instead of phone calls so that people associate you with
more than your voice. Or, consider picking a few important meetings,
such as staff retreats, and attending in person. When you are present,
be extra visible by greeting as many people as you can and sitting near
others. When you're working remotely, you could also consider being
slightly more active and responsive over instant messenger and in meetings (while still mirroring others), and offering more-regular status updates than you would if you were working in person.

**IF THERE ARE OPPORTUNITIES TO WORK WITH DIFFERENT PEOPLE,
SIGN UP.** Especially when compatibility doesn't come easily to you, use
your competence to kick the door open. Consider signing up for projects
involving people you haven't met yet or haven't been able to strike up a
conversation with. Large, cross-team (or even cross-office) projects and
initiatives can be efficient ways to expand your network. Start with work
talk, then sprinkle in some nonwork topics like, "How are you spending
the holidays?" and you'll be well on your way.

You could also volunteer for low-commitment activities that give you a
way to interact with people you wouldn't meet otherwise. An analyst at a
pharmaceutical company, for example, volunteered to lead her company's
university recruiting program. Within weeks, she was on a first-name
basis with several senior executives at the company. Like we discussed in

chapter 9, volunteering can be a powerful strategy, but it's important to be mindful of what you volunteer for. You only get credit for nice-to-do work if you're on top of your have-to-do tasks. And be mindful of the office housework trap if you are a woman or a person of color; unfortunately, office housework has a way of finding you.

When in doubt about whether to volunteer for something, ask a seasoned coworker you trust about the task. There may be a reason no one is signing up for something: it may be a project that all the experienced people know to avoid. Or, it could be a hidden opportunity that others don't recognize or need.

IF YOUR COWORKERS ORGANIZE SOCIAL EVENTS, CONSIDER JOINING, ESPECIALLY EARLY ON. A data scientist I interviewed told me about how someone who started at the same time he did ended up with more mentors and more-interesting assignments. It wasn't because the other person worked harder. It was because they met all the right people at work socials.

Things don't work this way everywhere, of course. Some teams have more of a social culture than others. One factor is your coworkers' stage of life. If your team and managers are mostly recent graduates, then expect more after-work parties (and the unspoken expectation that you will show up). If your team mostly consists of parents, then expect fewer socials—and more of a culture of people tuning out work after hours.

Either way, if there is a social event, consider showing up, at least for part of it—especially when you are new. The stronger your pattern of absence, the more your coworkers will assume that you are not interested, and the less likely they will be to invite you in the future. If you do attend, remember that you are still "at work" during these events, so act professionally and know your limits when it comes to alcohol. If you don't drink or don't want to drink, try ordering a soda, a nonalcoholic mixed drink, or sparkling water with lime. Hopefully, no one will make a big deal of your not drinking, but if someone does, try saying something like, "I have an early morning tomorrow, so need to make sure I'm on my A game" or simply, "I don't drink." That way, saying "no" to a social drink is framed in terms of your circumstances, rather than because you don't want to engage with your coworkers. And if you are underage, don't drink—besides being illegal, it may reflect badly on you with your superiors.

Play the Game

So, we've learned how to spark a conversation and keep our eyes open for opportunities and bids. Now we need to keep that imaginary tennis match going. This means hitting the ball smoothly over the net for the other side to hit back. Let's run through some tactics to make you an expert conversationalist.

Consider this example:

Joyce: "How was your weekend?"

Anand: "It was good."

Joyce: "What were you up to?"

Anand: "I hung out with some friends."

Joyce: "Cool! What kind of friends?"

Anand: "Some friends from my hometown."

   Silence

From Joyce's perspective, talking to Anand is like talking to a wall. If they were on a tennis court, it'd be as if Anand didn't hit the ball back. Here's a better example:

Joyce: "How was your weekend?"

Anand: "It was good! I had some friends in town. They've never seen Boston before, so it was fun bringing them around. What about you? What were you up to?"

Joyce: "I was sick, so I stayed home. Sounds like you had a good time?"

Anand: "Yeah, it was fun to catch up. But darn, sorry to hear that. There's definitely a bug going around. I was in bed all last weekend. Did you get some good rest at least?"

Joyce: "Yeah, luckily. Good thing it was the weekend. I'd hate to be sick this week."

Anand: "That's right! You have a big presentation, right? How are you feeling about it?"

Joyce: "Yes, good memory! I feel good, but that's only because of all the help you offered last week. Couldn't have done it without you."

If this version of Anand and Joyce's dialogue proves anything, it's that it is possible to have an entire conversation—and to lay the groundwork for a fruitful professional relationship—without much substance at all. All it takes is an effort to hit the ball back. Here are the tactics that both Joyce and Anand applied.

Contribute additional details. Joyce didn't have to mention that she was worried about being sick this week and Anand didn't have to talk about showing his friends around Boston, but both gave the other person something to latch on to.

Highlight commonalities. Even with a topic as minor as getting sick, commonalities are a surefire way of building compatibility. Talking about something that both sides are familiar with makes it easier for everyone to pull material into the conversation. For calls with people you cold emailed or were introduced to, research them online and look for any shared experiences, whether it's the same hometown, school, extracurricular activities, hobbies, or work history. Since you are asking for someone's time, the hidden expectation is that you will already know a bit about them and show up with a list of questions demonstrating that you've done your homework.

Focus on embracing over rejecting. It's easier to build on what others said than to disagree or drag others into a different topic. When in doubt, try what improv actors call "Yes, and . . .": accept whatever the other person just said, then add a comment that builds on their point.

Ask questions. Not only does this show your curiosity toward the other person, but it also gives them the chance to share more details, which you can, in turn, relate to and turn into a reply. This can be especially useful when you can't relate to the other person's experience and so cannot find any details to share about yourself. You don't always need to say, "Oh yeah! Me too!" It can be just as effective to say, "Oh yeah? Sounds interesting! How did that work?"

Listen. The more others see you as a listener and not an interrupter, the more they'll share—and the easier it will be to hold a conversation with them.

Balance your speaking time. No one wants to sit through a monologue, and no one wants to feel like they're talking to a wall. If you've been speaking a lot, consider asking a question. If you've mostly been asking questions, try adding more context behind your next question, commenting on the other person's reply, or introducing additional details about yourself.

Remember details. Everyone likes to feel important—and having others remember details about us is bound to feel good. Some good options to try are: "If I recall correctly, I believe you mentioned _____?" or "Didn't you say the other day that _____?" or "To your point earlier about _____ . . ."

Be uplifting. As a technology executive told me, "There are two types of people: energy givers and energy vampires. People don't like complainers—it just sucks the energy out of people. Be positive!" Although shared negative experiences can spark compatibility, consider letting others take the lead.

Remove all distractions. If you must multitask, share what you are about to do before you go ahead and do it. Often, all it takes is, "I'm sorry to be rude, but I'm expecting an email from my boss and just felt a vibration on my phone. Keep talking, I'm still listening."

Keep a smooth pace. Take too long a pause before speaking, and the conversation can get awkward. Don't take enough time, and you risk interrupting others—and sending the signal that you're just waiting for others to stop talking so you can start. So let others finish, then wait half a second before starting to speak yourself.

Mirror others. Pay attention to your conversation partner's speaking style and body language. Consider adopting a similar style. Doing so can help others see you as more compatible.

Wind the conversation down smoothly. To gracefully end the chat, try leaning back in your seat, standing up, or saying, "Don't let me keep you" or "Shall we?" Observe others' behavior also: if people are suddenly slowing down their replies, shifting around, summarizing the conversation, talking about next steps, or giving short answers, they may be trying to tell you to let them go.

But don't get me wrong: holding a smooth-flowing conversation with a stranger is hard work, especially if you don't have the same upbringing, experiences, and interests. Here's what an account manager at a media company told me: "My coworkers would talk about how they watched *The Bachelor* and took weekend trips to their cottages. My boss would be like, 'I'm taking my boat out on the lake this Saturday.' I stayed quiet because I didn't feel like I fit in. We came from different socioeconomic backgrounds. When my manager asked me, 'What are your plans this weekend?' and I said I was going to a hip-hop concert, she looked uninterested. After that, when people talked about their weekends, I just stayed quiet."

But when we spoke again a year later, he had realized that, while his manager could have found more-inclusive conversation topics, he could have done more to connect with others: "Your job isn't to simply do your job. It's also to build relationships. Networking can sound like a sleazy term, but it's just relationship building—and relationship building is essential if you want to succeed in your career. I could have shown interest by saying, 'I'm not familiar with the cottage life. What are your favorite activities?' or 'Oh, interesting, it reminds me of _____.'"

If you're panicking in a conversation and the last thing you can do is remember a long list of tips, consider an acronym an army captain taught me: Engage, Ask, Repeat, or EAR. *Engage* with what others have to say—listen, absorb, think. Then *ask* a question of your own. Finally, *repeat*—continue engaging and asking until you run out of things to talk about or until you have to get back to work. If you don't have much to relate to, focus on asking questions. Figure 11-1 shows the EAR cycle.

FIGURE 11-1

How to keep a conversation going

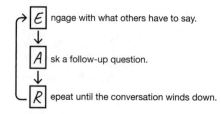

→ [*E*] ngage with what others have to say.

↓

[*A*] sk a follow-up question.

↓

[*R*] epeat until the conversation winds down.

Regardless of the tricks you use to keep the conversation flowing, remember: learning and applying a set of rules can get you only so far. There's no substitute for being genuine and sparking a conversation that both sides enjoy. So go ahead and do what you need to do to get started, but once you get the hang of things, throw all the rules away and focus on getting to know the other person. You've started the conversational tennis match. Now, keep hitting the ball back over the net!

Sustain the Momentum

Relationships aren't built from singular conversations. They're built from many interactions over many weeks and months. Now that we've reacted positively to bids and had a conversation or two, it's up to you to keep the relationship alive. Here are seven tactics to try, from least involved to most involved.

Say hi to them again. It's surprising how many people don't do this. Not acknowledging someone you've met can have an impact similar to saying, "I don't remember you." Give a hello, nod, smile, or "Nice to see you again." If you don't remember someone's name, try, "I'm so sorry, we went so quickly with our intros that I totally forgot your name. Mind reminding me again?"

Ask how things are going. A simple question like "How was your trip?" or "How did _____ end up going?" can be an easy way to signal that you were paying attention and that you care.

Share relevant news. Did you find an article, video, podcast episode, newsletter, or event that's relevant to someone? If so, forward them the link with "You may have already seen this, but it reminded me of our conversation." It's an easy way to signal that you're still thinking of them.

Offer an introduction. If you come across anyone who has similar interests or who might be helpful to the person you met, ask if they'd like an introduction. Then reach out to your contact to see if they'd be interested and, if so, become the broker of that double opt-in introduction we discussed earlier. You, too, can become a socialite—and an influencer.

Show gratitude. If someone gave you advice or help, send a thank-you email shortly after your meeting (ideally, the next day, but within a week at the latest). Not doing so, especially if you requested the conversation, can have an impact similar to saying, "I'm not grateful." Consider updating and thanking the person who brokered the introduction, too. Be generous with thank-yous. Make others feel good. Everyone appreciates the validation of "Thanks to you, I _____."

Mention you'd like to work together. When you're talking to someone who works on a team or project you'd like to join, try saying, "If you're in need of an extra pair of hands, please keep me in mind." You can't get what you don't ask for. Remember the mindset of *Let's give this a shot!*

Ask to grab lunch or coffee, or do a catch-up call. This approach can also work if you want a longer conversation, such as if you're interested in learning about their experiences (e.g., with grad school) or work (e.g., a prior project they led). But meetings can be burdensome, so make sure you have an idea of what you'd like to talk about, and consider reaching out to only a few people at a time so that you aren't seen as one of those aggressive networkers.

The strategies we discuss in this chapter aren't just relevant in a new job. They are relevant for any aspect of life, both professional and personal. And sometimes the line between personal and professional can blur.

This was what happened to Donovan, a laboratory technician in Toronto. Donovan told me how he built a large part of his personal network in a new city by answering people's bids while he was walking his dog at the nearby park. His dog helped, too. Whenever his pet tugged him toward another dog owner, Donovan would find an excuse to spark a conversation: "What's your dog's name? How long have you had her?" When he'd see the same people the following day, he'd ask about their week and how long they'd lived in the neighborhood. Before long, he was in a texting group with other 7 a.m. dog walkers, many of whom were in their thirties and forties.

Three years later, Donovan was looking to move to Houston and was on the job market. He was thinking about switching into real estate or work that was more tangible than laboratory work; he wanted to see and touch the product of his efforts. He shared his plans with several of his dog-owning friends. One of them offered to introduce Donovan to Karis, a family friend who worked in real estate in New York City. Even though he wasn't looking for jobs in New York City, Donovan accepted the introduction.

On the phone, Karis offered to pass Donovan's résumé on to Vicky, a college friend who worked in construction in Houston. After speaking with Vicky once over the phone, Donovan met with her and several of her coworkers over lunch after he arrived in Houston. Just as they were about to leave the restaurant, a friend of one of Vicky's coworkers—a superintendent at a construction company—walked by and started chatting with the group. Donovan introduced himself. Fast-forward, and while Vicky's company didn't end up having any open positions, Vicky's coworker had passed Donovan's résumé on to the superintendent of another construction company. A week later, Donovan was hired as a project manager.

If Donovan's story has taught me anything, it is that you never know where a relationship can take you, especially if you have the mindset of *Let's give this a shot.* In his case, you never know where a fifth-degree connection could take you. The first time for anything is always uncomfortable. This includes saying "Hello" to a stranger. But things always get easier the second, third, and fourth times around. Before long, that total stranger ends up becoming a familiar face, friendly acquaintance, supportive ally, or, in some cases, loyal champion. That coworker you didn't think you had anything in common with ends up leaving for a better opportunity—and taking you with them. That higher-up you didn't expect to say hello to ends up writing your reference letter. Start now! The earlier you set the virtuous circle of people and opportunities in motion, the more relationships you will build for yourself and the sooner opportunities will start emerging.

Try This

- Spark the connection: look out for and react positively to "bids"—requests from others for human connection; find excuses to offer bids; ask for introductions; cold email people; be present and be seen.

- Play the game: engage with what others have to say, ask questions, and repeat.

- Sustain the momentum: acknowledge others when you see them again and find ways to keep the conversation going and the relationship alive.

SECRETS TO

GETTING
AHEAD

Master Meetings

Peter, an analyst at a venture capital (VC) firm, had spent days preparing a research memo on a technology startup the firm was interested in investing in. There was a video call later that day with the startup's CEO; Peter would be joining his firm's managing partner, vice president (VP), and senior associate. Once he finished the memo, Peter sent the document to his colleagues and breathed a sigh of relief. He figured his work was done.

During the meeting, Peter's colleagues bombarded the CEO with questions about the startup's target market, partnership strategy, and hiring plan. Peter just listened on mute.

"Slide six shows a crowded market with lots of established players. What makes you different?" the managing partner asked.

"Slide twenty-six talks about your partnership strategy, but I'm not sure what all the arrows mean. Can you please explain?" the VP followed.

"What's your hiring plan for the next eighteen months?" the senior associate added.

After twenty-five minutes of nonstop questions, the managing partner motioned to Peter.

"We haven't heard from you yet. Any questions you want to ask?"

"Uh," Peter stammered. "Nope!"

"All right," the managing partner said to the startup's CEO. "That's it from our end. We'll be in touch."

Know This

- Meetings are opportunities for you to strategically demonstrate your competence, commitment, and compatibility.

- Demonstrating your Three Cs is all about knowing when you should be seen and heard, seen but not heard, and neither seen nor heard—and acting accordingly.

- The better you prepare, the better you will perform.

After the CEO dropped off the call, the VP spoke. "So, what do you all think? Should we invest in this company?"

"I have a question," the senior associate said. "She kept saying 'third party.' Did either of you catch what she was referring to?"

Peter's colleagues continued talking about what they liked and disliked about the company. Peter remained on mute. Finally the VP turned to him. "What do you think? You've been quiet."

Peter unmuted himself. "Uhh, I think it looks interesting. They seem like they have a lot of competitors, but they seem . . . interesting."

After the call, the managing partner instant messaged the VP:

> We need to talk about Peter. Does he not want to be here?

The VP replied:

> I can't tell. He did a good job with the research memo, though.

The managing partner replied:

> Was that really his work? Anyway, if he's good with memos, then give him the memos. But we can't have him taking up space like that.

From that point on, Peter went from being invited to video meetings to only being invited to phone calls.

What happened? We return to an unspoken rule we introduced in chapter 4: learner mode (when you don't know much yet, so people expect you to ask questions) versus leader mode (when people expect you to know what's going on and contribute to discussions). Peter fell below his coworkers' expectations on both fronts. He didn't ask questions when he was in learner mode and didn't speak up when he was in leader mode.

The lesson is this: People can't read your mind, so they don't know how hard you've been working or how good a job you've been doing. But they will observe how you come across in meetings (and in other settings)—and assume it fully and accurately reflects how you are doing in your job overall.

As we know, these judgments aren't always fair. Perhaps Peter didn't think it would be appropriate for him to speak up, given that he was the most junior person in the chain of command. Perhaps he didn't think his thoughts were important enough to share. Perhaps he was preoccupied with something else in his life, so he wasn't in the mood to contribute. Or perhaps others were faster to unmute themselves to speak, which left Peter flustered. No matter how positive Peter's intent may have been, his impact unfortunately ended up being negative.

And while the VP and managing partner could—and should—have asked Peter why he didn't speak up, they didn't. Instead, they relied on "We haven't heard from you yet. Any questions you want to ask?" and assumed that Peter would decode their subtle hint: *you should say something.*

Peter also could have done more. Namely, he could have asked for feedback on his participation (a topic that we will discuss in chapter 13). That way, he'd at least give his managers a chance to tell him what he needed to hear. But he didn't, and as a result, his career opportunities at the VC firm ended up being limited.

Let's make sure you don't end up in Peter's situation. Asking yourself seven questions can help you know what to do before, during, and after a meeting to amplify your Three Cs. Figure 12-1 shows what the questions are.

Before the Meeting

What will this meeting be about, and who will be in the room?

Over the course of a busy workweek, you may receive calendar invitations out of nowhere and requests like "Hey, can you come to this?" with

FIGURE 12-1

Seven questions to ask yourself to prepare for any meeting

When to ask

Before the meeting
{
What will this meeting be about and who will be in the room?

What's my role in this meeting?

What questions might I be asked?

What's my one thoughtful comment and one thoughtful question?
}

During
{
When should I speak up?

How can I best deliver my point?
}

After
{
What (if anything) do I need to do to follow up?
}

little explanation. Sometimes, your manager didn't have time to share the context with you. Other times, they mistakenly assumed you'd know something you actually don't. Whatever the reason, the unspoken expectation is that you'll know what the meeting is about—and be prepared.

There can be a bit of a double standard here. An engineer at a technology company told me how one of the firm's directors often entered meetings late, only to ask, "OK, what's this meeting about?" This comes back to the chain of command: the high-ranking director may have been able to pull this off, but you can bet they'd be prepared if their own boss were in the room.

So, it's often best to play it safe and be ready to contribute. Ideally, skim over any meeting agendas or calendar invitations as soon as you receive them. That way, you will know how important the meeting is, who else is attending (people outside your team, higher-ups, clients?), whether the spotlight will be on you, and how much you need to prepare, if at all. If you don't have access to this information, consider asking the person who invited you or a coworker at your level.

In general, meetings will be for either updates or discussions. Update meetings typically involve people taking turns sharing what they are working on and how things are going. Discussion meetings typically involve more free-flowing conversation. Despite the casual appearance,

FIGURE 12-2

The types of meetings you can expect at work

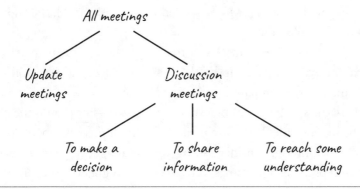

though, there's always a hidden goal—to make a decision, share information, or reach some understanding. Peter's story involved all three goals. The CEO meeting was for sharing information about the startup. The postmeeting debrief was for reaching some understanding around the startup's pros and cons. The conversation on instant messenger, which Peter didn't know about, was for making a decision on whether to invite Peter to future meetings. Figure 12-2 shows the different types of meetings.

The larger the meeting, the less speaking time each person will have—and the easier you will be able to "hide" without anyone noticing, especially if there are plenty of higher-ups present. However, if the meeting is small (say, under six or seven people), involves only your immediate coworkers, or is about a topic you've worked on, then the attention will likely be on you at some point. And that means you should stay alert—and consider spending time thinking about the following questions.

What's my role in this meeting?

As a junior employee, you can expect to play one of three unspoken roles in meetings:

BE BOTH SEEN AND HEARD. The meetings where you are expected to be both seen and heard are generally smaller, are internal to the team, or involve topics that you've been working on. The more work experience you have, the more knowledgeable you are on a certain topic, the less hierarchical a team you work for, and the smaller your meetings are (allowing for the spotlight to be shared among everyone), the more you will have this role in meetings.

This was also Peter's unspoken role: even though his firm was hierarchical, he was supposed to be the most knowledgeable person in the room, since he had prepared the research memo. He was also in a meeting where the spotlight was on everyone equally—not just on the person with the highest title. If you are invited to a small meeting about a project you are working on, consider asking your manager if there is anything you should prepare. Sometimes, your manager might even say, "You know what? *You* should present this. You are more familiar with the details anyway." And just like that, a new door of opportunity opened up.

BE SEEN BUT NOT HEARD. The meetings where you are expected to be seen but not heard are generally larger in-person meetings or videoconferences that involve more higher-ups, outside clients, or topics outside of your swimlane. You'll have this role more often if you work in a hierarchical environment where only the higher-ups speak in meetings. In these cases, everyone junior will usually sit quietly, listen, take notes, or speak only if asked. In more-hierarchical workplaces, often the more-junior people will sit by the wall or at the end of the table.

BE NEITHER SEEN NOR HEARD. The meetings where you are expected not to talk and not to be seen are typically conference calls where a higher-up in your organization speaks with a higher-up in another organization. In some cases, you might have two people speaking but a dozen people listening in on mute.

When this is your role, you may be expected to take notes that you will clean up and send to everyone after the meeting. If you aren't sure whether you are expected to perform such a role, consider asking your manager. And if you don't get a chance to ask, recognize patterns in what other coworkers at your level are doing—and mirror them. When you don't have to do anything but listen, enjoy the show: meetings can be a fun opportunity to read between the people.

Figure 12-3 shows the three kinds of roles you may have in meetings.

FIGURE 12-3

What you can expect to do in meetings

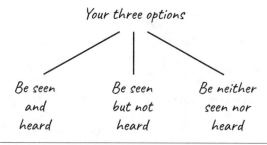

Your three options

Be seen
and
heard

Be seen
but not
heard

Be neither
seen nor
heard

No matter the type of meeting or your spoken responsibilities, you can generally expect at least two *unspoken* responsibilities: to learn (especially if you are new) and to represent your team (especially if you are the only person there from your team).

Here's an example of when someone was expected to learn—but didn't. A merchandising manager at a furniture company once told me about how she kept inviting her associate to negotiation meetings with suppliers. This manager had a certain style of negotiating and expected the associate to take notes and learn. But when the manager wanted the associate to lead the next negotiation, the associate asked, "What do I say?" In the words of this manager, "If you are in the room, I expect you to be learning. Why else did I invite you?!"

And here's an example of when someone was expected to represent. A business development representative (BDR) at a technology company once overheard managers from other teams discussing an upcoming cross-departmental meeting. This BDR reported the news back to her manager: "You may already know this, but I heard about a cross-functional go-to-market strategy meeting that I think overlaps with your vacation. I thought you might want to know in case you wanted to have our team represented."

It turned out that the manager didn't know about the meeting and it was, in fact, important. In the end, the manager found a replacement to attend for her—and invited the BDR to attend as well. You never know if your role in a meeting might lead to new opportunities, so don't be shy about speaking up if you have potentially valuable information.

What questions might I be asked?

Regardless of the meeting type, these three questions are all fair for others to ask you.

- What are you working on?

- What's the status of _____?

- Can you tell us more about _____?

Answering these questions confidently and concisely can be a great way to signal your competence and to leave people thinking, *Wow, this person really knows what they are talking about!* To make the best impression possible, consider reviewing all of your past, present, and future projects and mentally preparing to say the following sentences confidently.

- I'm working on _____, which is an effort to _____.

- So far I've done _____ and will focus on _____ next.

- I expect to finish _____ by _____.

- I could use some help with _____ because of _____.

- I know someone asked about _____ last time. I've looked into it and found out _____.

And if you have work on your computer that others might want to see, consider opening your files before the meeting so that you can quickly and confidently share your screen if you are asked. Gracefully being able to say, "Yes, happy to share. Here it is"—rather than stammering and fumbling like you don't have your work done—can be another subtle but effective way to signal that you have the situation under control.

What's my one thoughtful comment and one thoughtful question?

If you have time to prepare (and especially if a meeting includes anyone you'd like to impress), consider showing up with at least one thoughtful comment and one thoughtful question. This can be especially helpful if you struggle to think on your feet in meetings.

The word "thoughtful" may sound scary, but it just means that what you say should be important to the discussion *and* should highlight something missing, problematic, confusing, wrong, or unexpected. What's considered an "important" idea can depend on the goals of the meeting. If the goal is to make a decision, then any detail that might impact the decision could be important. If the goal is to share information or to reach an understanding, then anything that others might find interesting could be important.

Sometimes you will receive "prereads"—materials to read before the meeting. Try to read (or at least skim) them; the ingredients you need to cook up a thoughtful comment are buried somewhere in those materials. You can use the following questions to remind yourself of what to look for:

- What's missing?

- What's problematic?

- What's confusing?

- What's wrong?

- What's unexpected?

Any time you find something in the meeting materials that fits any of the above criteria, try writing it down. For important meetings involving clients and lots of details, it may take hours to prepare for a meeting. Often, however, this process takes less than thirty minutes. (This is why many people like to leave thirty-minute windows between meetings—to skim any materials so they show up with something intelligent to say.) Although you may not be expected to speak in meetings when you are new to a team (depending on the culture of your workplace), consider adopting the rule of one thoughtful comment and one thoughtful question anyway. It can't hurt: Even if you never get to make your comment or ask your question, the more informed you are, the better you will be able to follow the discussion. And the more you practice generating comments and questions, the faster you will get—and the less time you will need to budget for preparing for meetings in the future.

During the Meeting

If you are in a meeting where you are expected to be both seen and heard—or if you realize that you should speak up because everyone else at your level is doing it—then you'll need to know when and how to make your point.

When should I speak up?

In some meetings, especially larger ones, you may have only a single opportunity to speak up. Sometimes this opportunity will be nothing more than fifteen seconds where you're asked to introduce yourself (your external narrative). You'll want to make sure you do it—"Hi, my name is _____ and I am the _____ who is in charge of _____"—as clearly and confidently as possible. Make that single impression count. In other meetings, each person may be expected to speak multiple times, in which case a similar expectation will likely apply to you, too. Recognize the hidden pattern.

Timing can also be a strategic choice. The earlier you speak, the sooner you establish your presence and the more sway you may have over the tone and direction of the conversation—but you could also risk your point being forgotten later. The later you speak, the more sway you may have in the final decision—but you could also risk letting the discussion drift in a direction you might not agree with.

You will also want to carefully time your comment within the discussion. If you want to suggest that the team create a promotional video, consider bringing it up after the group has already warmed up to creating a marketing campaign. Suggest it too early, and people may be confused about why a video is even needed. Suggest it too late, after the group has moved on to talking about next year's budget, and you may have missed your opportunity.

Don't be shy about bringing new information to the meeting. Did you read an article, listen to a podcast, watch a video, or otherwise learn something (that isn't confidential) that can help people make a more informed decision? Consider mentioning it. Often, the most interesting comments are those from people who bring up relevant news or examples of what others are doing.

How can I best deliver my point?

Your goal here is not only to speak, but to be heard and remembered. This means speaking clearly, concisely, and confidently. First, think about whether your voice's pitch and tone indicate that you're making a statement or asking a question. When you're nervous, it can be easy to turn statements like "The back-up analysis is on page 16" (where you sound sure) into a question like "The back-up analysis is on page 16?" (where you sound *un*sure). Personally, I am still trying to overcome the habit of "asking questions" when I should be making statements.

Next, consider how you'll enter the discussion. Any of these phrases can help you connect your comment to what's been said so that people see the relevance:

- Agreed. Also . . .

- To _____'s point about _____ . . .

- Building on _____'s point . . .

- I like _____'s point about _____. This raises the question of _____.

- Following up on _____'s point . . .

If you are within a group of fast-talking extroverts or experienced co-workers, it can be overwhelming to both keep up *and* find something to say yourself. If you are blanking on ways to contribute, consider the following options.

- Contribute a relevant experience, comparison, or data point: "This reminds me of _____ where we _____ . . ."

- Point out an implication, contradiction, limitation, counterargument, or exception: "I like the idea, though it raises the question of _____ . . ."

- Offer the point of view of a stakeholder who hasn't been considered: "This makes sense from the perspective of _____, but from _____'s perspective . . ."

What to Do When Being Heard Is a Struggle

Meetings can be some of the most uneven playing fields in the workplace. Countless women have told me about their experiences of not getting called on to speak. And if they are called on, many are interrupted or ignored, or they make a point that a man repeats later in the meeting—and gets all of the credit for.

I've heard similar experiences from professionals who are racial minorities, nonnative speakers of the working language, or soft-spoken. Personally, I've struggled with managers who seemed to have selective hearing about my meeting contributions; these managers even complained about me never speaking up when they were the ones who weren't listening. If you find yourself fighting to be heard, it can be tiring—but know that your perspective matters. Keep trying. Here are a few ideas:

- If your meetings are being held over video chat, consider typing your idea in the chat window. While not everyone pays attention to what's being said, people do generally read and respond to what's written in the chat window.

- If you have a trusted coworker who is often heard, consider having them become a meeting ally or amplifier. They can call on you

- Introduce a framework to organize or summarize others' ideas or structure the question at hand: "What I'm hearing is there are three options: _____ . . ."

- Steer the group back to the main topic, to a prior decision, or to a decision on next steps: "Before we venture too far, I wanted to make sure that we _____ . . ."

Don't wait until you have the most brilliant comment to speak up. Your contribution doesn't have to win the Nobel Prize; it only has to nudge the group forward. I have to remind myself of this all the time. I think, *This idea is obvious, so I won't say it.* Then someone else makes my exact to speak, drop hints like, "As Ayane said" or "To Ayane's point," or gently remind the group that the idea everyone is praising actually came from you fifteen minutes ago.

- If a coworker takes credit for meeting materials that you made, consider putting your name on the document and being the one to email it to the group. That way, even if someone else is speaking, everyone can tell that you owned the work.

- If a manager or mentor encourages you to speak more often, consider sharing with them a topic you'd like to present on. Perhaps they can dedicate time for you to speak at an upcoming meeting. The more people hear you speak—and the more impressed they are when you do—the more they will seek out your opinion in the future.

If this section didn't seem to apply to you, the playing field may be tilted in your favor. But with privilege comes responsibility. If you find that someone on your team isn't heard as easily as you are, consider being an ally or amplifier yourself. You have an opportunity to make an impact.

comment and gets all the credit. Or I spend minutes polishing the perfect comment in my head, only for someone else to say something unpolished but useful. Lower your standards. Asking a question can often be just as impactful as making a statement. As long as your question helps the group clarify something and you frame your questions using the structure, "Here's my question, and here's why I'm asking it" or "Here's what I know, and here's what I don't know," it is unlikely that anyone will accuse you of asking a stupid question.

Once you start delivering your message, be mindful of how you look and sound. It's tempting to speak quickly when you're nervous. If this is your tendency, then speak half . . . as quickly as . . . you want to. You'll sound clearer and more confident that way. It's also easy to look down or up, sink in your chair, fiddle with your pen, play with your hair or facial hair, or get jittery. If any of these are your tendency, try to keep your eye contact steady, either by looking at the person you're speaking to or by glancing at one person and holding their gaze for a second before moving on to the next person. Sit up straight in your chair and gesture slowly and smoothly. If you are on the phone and speak more confidently when you are standing up, consider standing for the call.

After the Meeting

What (if anything) do I need to do to follow up?

The meeting may be over when everyone drops off the call or leaves the room, but the opportunity to flex your Three Cs continues. Is there anything you need to clarify? Or were you quiet in the meeting and need to reinforce your commitment with your manager? If so, try asking some follow-up questions, using the approach we discussed in chapter 3 of *do—and show—your homework*.

Was there a task that was implicitly or explicitly assigned to you? Repeat back what you heard to whomever you need to work with, saying, "Just to recap, would it make sense if I did _____ next?" as we discussed in chapter 8.

Is the group expecting your meeting notes or meeting summary? If so, edit your notes; check your spelling, grammar, and formatting; attach any relevant files; and send it off. Include a bullet-point list of decisions made, next steps, owners of each task, and deadlines.

Was there someone in the meeting you'd like to get to know, learn from, or stay in touch with? Try sending them a message with "Nice meeting you earlier in the discussion about _____. Looking forward to working with you" or any of the options we discussed in chapter 11. Being in the same meeting is enough of an excuse to follow up with someone. Consider whether you need to build a stronger relationship with your own manager and teammates also. A quick question like "How do you think that meeting went?" can sometimes be enough to spark a conversation.

Follow-ups aren't required—or even advised—in every case, of course. Perhaps this was one of those meetings that should have been an email.

Perhaps this meeting was held only to make some higher-up happy. Perhaps all the men are subconsciously waiting for a woman to volunteer for the office housework. If doing nothing is your best option, do nothing.

What to Do When You Are in Charge

Just as you can expect to transition from learner mode to leader mode as you establish your Three Cs, you can also expect to transition from attending meetings to organizing them. Sometimes, these meetings will be casual check-ins with your managers and team. Other times—especially if you work in a small organization like a startup—you may be expected to lead entire meetings with other departments or even clients. If you find yourself in organizer mode, consider the following seven steps:

Determine the objective and agenda. Picture what success looks like, then work backward: What decisions do you want to have made by the end of the meeting? What topics do you want to have discussed? Consider listing the goals, questions for discussion, or meeting agenda, and sharing them so people don't complain that this is another meeting that could have been an email.

Pick the attendees. Consider your RACI list. Who needs to be present for the decision to happen? Who should be invited out of courtesy, even if they don't attend? For higher-ups, who might prefer to schedule through their assistants? When in doubt, ask your manager.

Decide the time, location, and meeting method. When is everyone available? (Mind your time zones!) What medium works best (in person, video, or phone call)? Try polling your participants, looking at calendars, or just deciding yourself, then send a calendar invitation. Keep the meeting to the minimum length possible.

Share the prereads and prework. Are there any documents that people should read or surveys to take ahead of time? Do you want people to come with ideas? Consider what people can do on their own to make the meeting more productive, then share the directions with the group. If you need someone to speak up or take notes, ask them ahead of time so that they agree and are prepared.

Set the stage. What will you say at the start of the meeting to help people understand its broader objective? What tone would you like to establish? If you tend to get nervous, consider writing out some bullet points and asking your manager for feedback.

Keep people on track. As the "chair" of the meeting, your primary job is to make sure you get through the entire agenda. So, be ready to keep an eye on the time, keep people focused on the agenda and broader goals, and redirect the group if people get sidetracked.

Clarify the next steps. Similar to repeating back instructions when receiving a task, reserve time near the end of the meeting to clarify decisions that were made and who is responsible for doing what next. Consider sending meeting "minutes" (notes) if needed.

In the end, mastering meetings is as much about projecting competence, commitment, and compatibility as it is about reminding yourself of your role. Here is what an executive recruiter told me: "Understanding and knowledge are more valuable than simply pretending and getting through the meeting. Pretending may work in the short run, but the people who ask the right questions and learn will eventually overtake you. Rather than pretend, be honest when you don't know. Being curious, teachable, and self-aware is more important than being perfect." In other words, the end goal is not simply to be noticed, but to be curious, to learn, and to contribute. The fact that you've gotten this far in this guide means you already have such a mindset. Just don't forget to bring the mindset with you to your next meeting.

Another caveat: keep in mind that the strategies in this chapter (and the book more broadly) are just a starting point. There may be times when it's best to speak in a meeting, even if you think your role is to be seen but not heard. There may be times when it's best to speak a few times, even if others only speak once. There may even be times when you should come up with a reasonable excuse to skip a certain meeting because you don't need to be there or you have more important things to get done. Go ahead and play by the rules—but don't forget that you are following them only so you can bend or even reject them later. Don't let some stuffy old ways of doing things prevent you from doing your best work.

Try This

- Before joining a meeting, understand what it will be about and who will be in the room.

- Figure out what your unspoken role should be in any meeting: Should you be both seen and heard? Seen but not heard? Or neither seen nor heard?

- Brainstorm a list of questions you could be asked, along with potential answers.

- Come up with at least one thoughtful comment and question based on any outside information or anything that's missing, problematic, confusing, wrong, or unexpected in the prereads.

- Time your comment for when it will most likely be embraced.

- Be deliberate about how you contribute to the discussion.

- Strategically follow up after meetings to reinforce your Three Cs.

- When organizing meetings, carefully consider your meeting objective and agenda; attendees; time, location, or meeting method; prereads and prework; introduction; meeting orchestration; and postmeeting follow-ups.

Manage Feedback

The best managers will typically give you feedback clearly and frequently. Many managers, however, won't do this at all. But just because your manager doesn't say anything about your performance doesn't mean they don't have anything to say. They know what you need to do—to keep your job, get promoted, or turn your internship or temp position into a full-time role.

Given that your manager is the person who stands between where you are and where you want to go, it's critical to know how they feel about your work and your future in the organization. The sooner you find out, the more time you have to improve. Let's discuss how to decode what your manager is thinking, so that you are always in control.

How to Decode Your Manager

Much of the feedback you will receive at work will be in the form of offhand remarks and body language from your manager, rather than formal report cards as we are familiar with from school. When you're starting out, it's possible you may also receive feedback from anyone you are paired up with (say, the supervisor of your summer project). The feedback you receive will come in two ranges: from verbal to nonverbal and from direct to indirect.

Know This

- Grades and report cards don't exist in the workplace as they do in school.

- To understand how you're performing at work, you'll need to get good at asking for, interpreting, and adapting to others' feedback.

How direct or indirect you can expect your manager's feedback to be can depend on how confrontational your manager is, what type of culture your team has, and, according to INSEAD professor Erin Meyer, which country you're in (or which country's working culture your manager is most familiar with).[1] If you work in "direct" countries like Russia, Israel, or Germany, or have a manager who is used to direct cultures, then you may get criticized frankly, bluntly, and even in front of others. If you're in "indirect" countries like Japan, China, or Indonesia, or your manager is used to their working cultures, then you may receive feedback that's more toned down, at least on the surface. Here's what a project manager who has worked in both Russia and the United States told me:

People in the United States are so much less direct with feedback than people in Russia. In Russia my boss would yell, "What were you thinking when you put these slides together?! Do you even understand what you are doing? Come back in two hours with a deck [presentation] that's clearer." In the United States my boss would say, "I think you did a great job putting this together. Let's maybe think about how to make it crisper. What if we tried to change the message here? What do you think of this?" There are pros and cons to both styles. American-style feedback might be more helpful and productive in the moment, but if you're not careful you could end up mistakenly believing that you did a good job when you actually sucked.

How you should interpret what people say can also depend on where you work. Some countries, such as the United States, Canada, Australia, the Netherlands, and Germany, are considered "low-context," while others, such as Japan, Korea, Indonesia, China, and Kenya, are considered "high-context."[2] In low-context cultures, you can generally take others' words at face value because people say what they mean. In high-context cultures, you need to rely on what's unspoken and consider others' body language, facial expressions, and relationship to you, as well as the dynamics of the situation. Here's what a Ghanaian marketing manager told me about his experience working with Germans (who are lower-context) and Ghanaians (who are higher-context):

> One time, my German clients asked, "Can we go to the local market on our own?" And I said, "Sure, you could . . ." and they turned around and left for the market. Once they heard "sure," they immediately concluded that the situation was fine without reading my nonverbal cues. A local, on the other hand, would hear the "could," see my squinting eyes and pursed lips, and immediately know that I really meant, "No, I would not advise that." Of course I meant "no"! I left a silence before the "sure" and had an upward inflection in my voice. I wasn't nodding. And their idea was completely ridiculous to begin with.

This is not to say that all Germans or all Ghanaians communicate in similar ways, though. As business becomes increasingly global, you may encounter managers and coworkers who shift between communication styles without realizing it. If you aren't careful and jump to conclusions about how someone communicates, you could, like the Germans in the quote, wander off when your manager really wanted you to stay put (or vice versa).

Since feedback can get confusing on the indirect and high-context side and uncomfortable on the direct and low-context side, let's discuss what each of these types of feedback sounds like and looks like—and what you can do if you encounter each style (or a combination of styles). Figure 13-1 shows how they compare.

Subtle hints (indirect and verbal)

This is the type of feedback that sometimes doesn't feel like feedback at all. Often, it'll sound like lukewarm approval ("Yeah, maybe . . ."), gentle suggestions ("What about this?"), or anxious questions ("How's your work coming along?"). It represents whatever your manager wants to say to you,

FIGURE 13-1

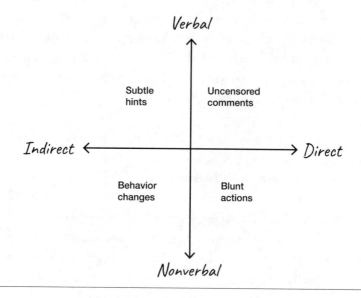

The ranges of feedback you can expect in the workplace

but diluted down to something more polite and gentle. But although your manager's "How's progress on the project?" may sound polite, they may be thinking something like *You're so slow, come on, speed it up!* They may simply be self-censoring so they'll seem kinder and more understanding.

A software engineer I interviewed experienced exactly this type of feedback. Throughout her summer internship, her manager kept saying, "It would be great if . . ." and "How about we try . . ." and asking questions like, "Are you doing OK?" and "Any updates?" When she discussed her work with her manager, he'd respond with nothing more than, "OK . . ." and "Hmm . . ." It wasn't until her last day—after learning that she wasn't being offered a full-time job—that she realized her manager had actually been complaining behind her back about her working too slowly. In this software engineer's words, "He never gave his opinion—and I never asked. I really had no clue until it was too late."

Since it can sometimes be difficult to interpret the intent behind your manager's impact, it can be helpful to transform subtle cues into a less subtle form. One option is to ask, "When you say _____, do you mean _____ or something else?" Another option is to ask for feedback regularly, which we will discuss shortly. Or, if you don't have the chance to clarify or ask for feedback, you can consider playing it safe and treating even minor suggestions as commands and then gauging your manager's reactions.

Uncensored comments (direct and verbal)

These are the undiluted version of subtle hints. This is the type of feedback where managers don't just think *You're so slow, come on, speed it up!*—they say exactly that. At their best, uncensored comments are exactly the type of feedback you want: clear and to the point. However, at their worst, uncensored comments can be far from polite.

An investment banking analyst I interviewed received uncensored comments from one of her managers, who would yell things like, "Look at this: it says 8.3 on this page and 6.3 on this other page. How can you not check your numbers? Are you incompetent?!"

Whereas subtle hints can be difficult because their intent can be unclear, uncensored comments can be difficult because their impact can hurt. Imagine being told—potentially in front of everyone—"That's dumb," "This is garbage," or "Stop talking." If you get direct feedback, it helps to uncover the root cause of your manager's behavior. Could their comments be the result of them not having any luck with their subtle hints? Could they be struggling to control their stress? Could they not be aware of the negative impact of their positive intent? Or, could they have been trained in a direct working culture?

An American intern who worked in Israel—a country known for its direct feedback culture—told me he once was rattled to hear two coworkers screaming at each other in the company kitchen. He snuck behind the doorway to eavesdrop, only to realize they were arguing over the type of coffee to put in the coffee machine. They fought and fought, decided on the coffee, and then went back to work like nothing happened. None of their local coworkers even flinched. From this American intern's perspective, his coworkers needed to tone it down; from his coworkers' perspective, however, this American intern needed to toughen up.

When in doubt, consider asking for advice from a colleague who has worked with your manager before. The investment banking analyst I interviewed suggested focusing on *what* your manager is trying to say,

Beware of Bias (Again)

An account manager wondered if he was truly fired because he sent the wrong file to a client one too many times—or because he was scrutinized more as the only Black man in a predominantly white workplace. A policy analyst wondered if she really was "aggressive"—or if that label meant she was defying gender stereotypes as the only woman to speak up within a group of men. A private equity associate wondered if she wasn't assigned higher-profile projects because she needed to improve her financial analysis skills—or because she had an accent.

As much as managers may claim to evaluate you on your competence, we know that it's also about commitment and especially compatibility. The workplace is far from a perfect institution. And as we can tell from this chapter, feedback in the workplace is far from a perfect process. Look for allies. Find people who've been in your shoes and ask them for advice. You may not know that senior associate from the other team, but if they've worked with your manager before, they've gone through the trial and error so you don't have to.

rather than *how* they say it: "I cut through his anger to get to the substance of his feedback, which was to show more attention to detail. The substance of your manager's feedback may be productive, even though their communication style is unproductive."

If your manager's directness is making you uncomfortable, it's worth having a conversation. We will go into more detail on how to approach such a conversation in the next chapter.

Behavior changes (indirect and nonverbal)

This is the type of feedback where managers think *You're so slow, come on, speed it up!* but instead of saying it to your face, they suddenly start setting up more-frequent meetings or micromanaging you (actions that may indicate dissatisfaction with the speed or quality of your work). Or, your manager might suddenly start avoiding you with no explanation (which, unless they are busy, may indicate that they've given up).

A former coworker of mine always made typos. His manager had told him several times to be more "careful" and to "show more attention to detail." This coworker never clarified what "careful" or "attention to detail" meant, so he didn't do anything differently. After seeing no improvement for several weeks, his manager simply stopped giving him work—and tried to move him to another team. Like subtle hints, behavior changes can be tricky because we can't read others' minds, so it can be hard to uncover the intent behind the impact: *Is my manager excluding me because I messed up—or because he didn't want to waste my time? Is my manager pulling me from this meeting because I was inappropriately dressed—or because he wants to keep the meeting small? Is my manager not giving me work because there's no work to do—or because he doesn't trust me?*

It will take time to figure out your manager's quirks. It took a program manager I interviewed over five years of working with a certain director to decipher when a lack of email response from the director meant "No" and when it meant "I've forgotten to respond, so please remind me again." Until then, be sensitive to sudden changes in others' patterns of behavior—and try to figure out why they are happening. What events led up to the sudden change? Try to retrace your steps to see if there was anything you did or didn't do. Or, confront it head-on with a comment like, "I've noticed _____ lately, which worries me because _____. Can we chat?"

Blunt actions (direct and nonverbal)

This is the type of feedback where managers think *You're so slow, come on, speed it up!* and, rather than saying it, show it by diverting work that is normally yours to someone else. Or, on the extreme end, they might throw out your work in front of you, or stomp up to you and refuse to walk away until a task is done.

I had one of these managers once. As I was fixing a technical glitch before a presentation, my manager stormed up to me, his dress shoes clacking on the hardwood floor. He left only about a palm's width between his nose and mine. He inhaled and pursed his lips. "We need this fixed. Now." Thank goodness that only happened one time.

Given that it's rare for managers to show nonverbal cues without also saying something direct, much of what we discussed in the

Why Is Feedback So Difficult?

Humans care a great deal about being liked and like to think highly of themselves. But since criticism threatens the glowing self-image we have, delivering it is hardly a sure way to make friends. Our brains are wired with a defense mechanism that reacts more strongly to negative experiences (like criticism) than to positive experiences (like praise).[a] So, as much as managers say they want to be good mentors, and as much as employees say they want critical feedback, the reality is that most managers dread giving negative feedback as much as employees dread receiving it.[b] The result? We keep looking for what we want to hear, rather than what we need to hear. And our managers keep telling us what we want to hear, rather than what we need to hear. Over time, they find it increasingly difficult to give critical feedback—while we find it increasingly difficult to receive it. Have empathy for your manager. Like you, they are trying their best.

a. Roy F. Baumeister et al., "Bad Is Stronger Than Good," *Review of General Psychology* 5, no. 4 (2001): 323–370.

b. Jack Zenger and Joseph Folkman, "Why Do So Many Managers Avoid Giving Praise?," hbr.org, May 2, 2017, https://hbr.org/2017/05/why-do-so-many -managers-avoid-giving-praise; Paul Green Jr. et al., "Shopping for Confirmation: How Disconfirming Feedback Shapes Social Networks," working paper 18-028, Harvard Business School, Boston, 2017.

uncensored-comments section applies here, too. Try to see the intent behind the impact. At the same time, reflect on how these actions make you feel and whether working around such a pattern of behavior is sustainable. Not all feedback is productive feedback. Not all managers are good managers.

How to Ask for Feedback

Decoding your manager is a good start, but it is still a guessing game. Nothing beats asking for feedback—and having your manager tell you directly where you can improve. Let's walk through how to ask for and then respond to feedback.

If you already have regular meetings with your manager, you're well on your way. The next step is to simply introduce feedback into the conversation. But if you aren't already meeting with your manager on a regular basis, then consider asking, "Would you have a few minutes to chat in the coming days? I'd love to hear how I am doing and if there is any way I can improve in my work." Here are some tactics for making the most of that meeting.

Before the meeting

Feedback meetings are still work meetings, so it's important to keep an eye on your Three Cs. This means knowing what you want to say and ask. Think one step ahead and mentally rehearse answers to the following questions, which are likely to come up. I've included some sample responses to get you started (though feel free to get creative and make them your own).

> **"How are things going?"** "Things are going _____. I am grateful for _____ and have enjoyed working on _____. That said, I am trying to improve my _____ and could use your help."

> **"How are things going with [some specific project]?"** "Things are going _____. So far I've done _____, but I am not yet done with / am not sure about / could use your help with / am struggling with / am looking forward to working on _____."

> **"Do you have any feedback for me?"** "It's been great working with you. If I had to pick something, I'd say that it'd be helpful to _____. This might just be a personal preference, but I've often found it helpful when _____."

> **"Where do you see yourself in the future?"** "I can definitely see myself working here long term and would love your advice on how I can get more involved with _____." (This is useful if you are interested in staying and growing with the organization.) You might also try, "I am still deciding, but so far I've loved working with _____ on _____ and would love to get your advice on _____." (This is helpful if you aren't sure your role

is right for you, but don't want your manager questioning your commitment.)

While some managers will stick to the unspoken agenda and spend feedback meetings giving you feedback, not all managers will. Some managers will instead treat the meeting as a progress-update meeting. If this happens to you, you'll want to get your manager back on track using some of the prompts below. But to play it safe and give your manager what they want, consider reviewing chapter 12 so that you are prepared to speak about what you are working on, what the status is, and what you plan to do next.

During the meeting

As is the case with many meetings in the professional world, expect to start with small-talk questions such as "How's your day been so far?" or "How's your week looking?" or "How was your weekend?" Then, set the stage by thanking your manager for their time, talking about how you value their opinion, and framing the discussion in terms of you wanting to improve. You could say, for example, "Thanks for taking the time to chat. I value your opinion a lot and would love to talk about anything I can do to improve and take my work to the next level." Here are some questions to get you started.

- "What should I start doing? Stop doing? Keep doing?"[3]

- "Am I on track with [whatever project I've been assigned]?"

- "Am I on track to [receive a full-time job offer or get promoted]?"

If you aren't satisfied with what you're hearing, try pushing gently with some follow-up questions:

> **If you receive critical feedback that's not specific enough.** "Interesting. Can you share any specific moments when I _____?"

> **If you aren't sure how to apply certain feedback.** "Good point. I'd love to _____. Any suggestions on how I can apply this feedback going forward?"

If you receive feedback that's difficult to apply. "That's a good point. How would you suggest I balance _____ with _____?"

If you receive feedback you disagree with and you want to explain yourself. "Thanks for that. I could definitely improve on _____. I'm just thinking back to that moment and wonder if what went through my head was _____."

If you want help achieving a certain goal. "I'd love to _____ and would appreciate your advice. How would you suggest I go about navigating _____?"

When you don't know what to say next. "I appreciate you bringing that up."/"That's a good point."/"That's interesting."/"That's helpful."/"Thanks for that."

Remember the unspoken rule of sending the right signals: nod and take notes during the meeting, and consider taking notes by hand if you are meeting in person, to send the signal that you are focused and serious.

If you made a mistake—or if your manager believes you did—consider playing it safe and owning up. If you can feel your frustration or anxiety building, try to avoid sighing, raising your voice, or rolling your eyes. Breathe calmly. Instead of disagreeing, try asking for clarification. Then, toward the end of the meeting, repeat back what you think you heard and clarify next steps. You could say, for example, "Thanks for this. In terms of next steps, would it make sense if I _____, or did you have something else in mind?" You could also add, "I'd love to make this a more regular conversation if you have time. Would you be open to me setting a recurring calendar invite?"

Feedback meetings don't have to only be about your current job or whatever your manager wants to discuss. They can also be hidden opportunities for you to help your manager help you. Here are a few questions to consider asking:

To get involved with something new. "I noticed that _____ recently announced a new _____ initiative. I'd love to be more involved given _____. Do you have any ideas on how I can put my name forward?"

To do more work that you enjoy. "The more I think about / work on _____, the more interested I am in _____. How can I position myself to do more of this work?"

To obtain your manager's support for an opportunity. "I came across _____, a program aimed at _____, and that aligns with my interest in _____. The form asks for references who can speak to my _____. Would you be open to supporting my candidacy? I will need _____, which I can make easier by _____."

These questions don't quite work when you are new and still trying to establish your Three Cs, but if you've been getting consistently positive feedback, don't be shy about making one-on-ones work for you. Good managers will want to see you succeed. But even the best managers can't read your mind, so they won't know how to support you unless you tell them what you want.

After the meeting

Try to apply the feedback you received as soon as possible—and especially when your manager is around. The longer you wait, the stronger a signal you send that you weren't listening. Even if you don't agree with the feedback you've been given, consider applying it anyway—at least to signal your commitment and compatibility. Then consider reporting back to your manager with your progress to show that you are taking their advice seriously.

If you attempt to apply their feedback, but realize that it is unreasonable or infeasible, you could report back and say, "I've been trying to apply your advice to _____, but have been struggling with _____. Do you have any advice on how to better navigate these situations?" If the feedback ends up being helpful, however, you could report back with, "Thanks so much for your suggestion to _____. I've been trying it on _____ and _____ occasions and have seen _____ improvements."

In the end, it's often not about how positive or negative the feedback is, but rather about how readily you embrace and apply it. Kayode, a new high school teacher, taught me this lesson through a story from his experience. The assistant principal at his school, Angela, had a habit of asking all teachers to create a "word wall," a classroom bulletin board displaying all the vocabulary words from the course. Many teachers at the school saw the exercise as a waste of time.

One time, Angela walked into the classroom of Carl, another new teacher. Within seconds, Angela noticed the absence of a word wall.

"Carl," Angela said, "have you considered creating a word wall?"

"I'll look into it," Carl replied dismissively.

Angela then walked into Kayode's classroom and made the same comment: "Kayode, have you considered creating a word wall?"

Fast-forward one week, and Kayode had created the word wall. He even invited Angela to visit his classroom to check it out. And when Angela was in Kayode's classroom, he made an extra effort to refer students to the word wall, just to show that he was using it. Angela was clearly pleased. After class, she walked by Carl's classroom. Carl still didn't have a word wall.

At the following week's staff meeting, Angela had another classroom activity called a "write-around," which many of the teachers, once again, saw as a waste of time. However, this time, Angela's gaze was squarely fixed on Carl, who was leaning back in his chair with his arms crossed.

"Carl, I want to see you try a write-around."

Carl clicked his tongue. "I've already done a write-around. Write-arounds are stupid."

Angela's face turned bright red.

Kayode had done a write-around before and secretly thought it would be pointless—but he tried it anyway. And, as expected, it didn't work. But the next time Kayode saw Angela, he said, "I tried the activity you suggested. I like the idea a lot, but found that my students started tuning out. Do you have any advice on how to navigate this?"

Angela smiled. "Oh, that's OK. It doesn't always work. I'm glad you tried!"

Later on, Kayode was promoted to department head. Carl didn't pass his probation period and was fired after his first year. Looking back, Kayode told me:

> *I can see where Carl is coming from. As a new teacher, you are already putting in eighty-hour weeks. You're exhausted, and here comes your*

boss telling you to do something that you don't think is useful. But it's worth it: all I had to do was spend forty-five minutes taping colored pieces of paper to the wall to show that I was coachable and open to feedback. Carl got more-aggressive feedback over time. I got less-aggressive feedback over time. Angela and I liked each other more and more; Angela and Carl liked each other less and less. And it all started from me taking Angela's feedback and Carl being defiant and constantly signaling that he didn't respect her.

The spoken objective of a feedback meeting may be to help you improve, but the unspoken objective is to help your manager feel validated. It's hardly about how right you think you are or even how right you really are; it's about *how right your manager thinks they are*. When it comes to feedback, it's not about what's "right" and what's "wrong"; it's about what aligns with your manager's worldview and working style and what doesn't. All feedback is subjective. Own it and move on.

Whether the feedback you receive reflects a true area of improvement or your manager's own needs and wants, navigating feedback is a skill—and one that will benefit you for the rest of your career. No matter if it's good or bad, all feedback is "good" feedback, at least in terms of helping you to learn and grow (and, if nothing else, to understand who to work with and who to avoid). As is the case with all of the topics in this book, remember how you feel. You may be on the receiving end of feedback now, but it's only a matter of time before you'll be on the giving end. Think about the experience you would have wanted—and create it for the next person who works for you. We can all do our part to make feedback a less imperfect process.

Try This

- Ask your manager for feedback on a regular basis if you aren't receiving any.

- Be sensitive to your manager's lukewarm approvals, gentle suggestions, and anxious questions—it may be feedback.

- Try to see the intent behind the impact of any rude remarks and actions from your manager—what are they trying to communicate?

- Retrace the events leading up to any sudden changes in behavior from your manager, and consult a trusted coworker for advice about what it may mean.

- Remember that feedback is rarely about what's right and what's wrong; often, it's about what aligns with your manager's worldview and working style.

Resolve Conflicts

Despite your best efforts to maximize your Three Cs, sometimes something just doesn't feel right. Maybe you are anxious. Or frustrated. Or exhausted. If and when these emotions cross your mind, you have three options: fix the situation, live with the situation, or leave the situation. Figure 14-1 shows these options.

Picking what to do and how to do it matters. Sometimes, it could even be the difference between addressing the problem and not.

Kathryn, a consultant, learned this lesson the hard way. When her favorite manager left for another company, Kathryn began reporting to a senior director whose management style was totally different from what she was used to. Her prior manager always let her lead client meetings and take on new responsibilities that helped her learn and grow. Her new manager kept her behind the computer and away from clients. Her prior manager rarely asked her to travel (which she appreciated), and when she did, allowed her to return home on Fridays. Her new manager sent her on weeklong projects, even though the clients were rarely around. Her prior manager regularly held heart-to-heart conversations with her, becoming more of a mentor than a manager. Not once did her new manager reach out to her to chat. Within weeks, Kathryn went from loving work to lacking the motivation to get out of bed. Through a friend, she found a new job at an asset management company.

Know This

- When things don't go your way at work, you have three options: live with the situation, fix the situation, or leave the situation.

- Your ability to fix the problem relies on your ability to diagnose the problem.

When she started work, however, she quickly discovered that the new job was not what she had expected. In her old job, there were executives she could look up to as role models, but her new job didn't have anyone like that. Kathryn may have been unhappy about the sudden lack of mentorship at her old company, but she was even less happy at her new firm.

Kathryn lasted only nine months before leaving. She took a job at a smaller firm, but it, too, wasn't perfect. Less than a year later, Kathryn quit and returned to her original consulting firm. Luckily, her company was open to "boomerang employees"—people who leave, work somewhere else, and then return. Though Kathryn was satisfied in the end, she returned at the same level and pay as when she left. In that time, many of her coworkers in her starting cohort had already been promoted to manager.

Kathryn abruptly decided that she couldn't live with the situation, so she would leave without first trying to fix it. She thought she knew what

FIGURE 14-1

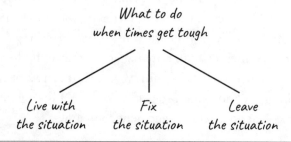

Your options for responding to a difficult situation at work

What to do
when times get tough

Live with   Fix   Leave
the situation   the situation   the situation

she was running away from, but hadn't fully grasped what she was leaving behind. And she knew she was running toward something, but hadn't fully grasped what she was signing up for. As a result, she spent two years chasing greener grass, only to realize that the grass was greenest where she began.

How can you avoid ending up in Kathryn's situation when confronting challenges at work? Don't just pursue the path of fastest relief or of least effort; pursue the path of least regret. Although every situation is different, a helpful rule of thumb is to diagnose the problem, evaluate your options, and fix the problem tactfully—or, if the situation warrants it, leave graciously. Let's discuss what each step entails.

Step 1: Diagnose the Problem

If things don't feel quite right, the first step is figuring out the root cause—the hidden problem that is causing the racing thoughts, sleepless nights, or lack of motivation. When it comes to workplace challenges, root causes often come in three general flavors. Figure 14-2 shows what these flavors are.

> **People problems.** If you have an issue with a particular manager, coworker, or client, then you have a people problem. An engineer had a coworker who always appeared in the final moments of a project to take credit for her work. She had a *people* problem.

FIGURE 14-2

Potential root causes of your problem

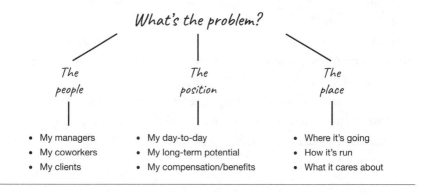

What's the problem?

The people	The position	The place
• My managers • My coworkers • My clients	• My day-to-day • My long-term potential • My compensation/benefits	• Where it's going • How it's run • What it cares about

Position problems. If you dislike your day-to-day work, are worried about your long-term career, or are frustrated by low pay or lack of benefits, then you have a position problem. A psychology research associate lost interest in his job because there didn't seem to be a clear career path for him at the research institute. He had a *position* problem.

Place problems. If you are frustrated or worried about where your organization is going, how it is run, or what it cares about, then you have a place problem. A public policy analyst was assigned more and more work as some of her coworkers quit, but she wasn't offered more pay or support, or even training to do her work. She had a *place* problem.

How to find the root cause

To find the root cause of your struggle, consider using the problem-solving approach we discussed in chapter 9: keep asking, "Why is this happening?"

Here is how Kathryn's "Why?" exercise could have unfolded:

I am feeling zero motivation to go to work.

Why?

Because I don't enjoy my time there as much as I used to.

Why?

Because the people aren't as great to be around.

Why?

Because I'm working with a different manager with a different working style.

Aha!

Looking back, the root cause of Kathryn's problem wasn't *everything*—it was her new manager. The boring work, the overwhelming travel, and the poor mentorship may have felt like different problems, but they were all symptoms with a single root cause.

Not all root causes will be immediately obvious. They can sometimes take weeks and months to uncover. If you are struggling to identify the root cause of your issue, consider ending each day by journaling about a few questions:

- What did you do today?

- What did you learn today?

- How did you feel at different points in the day? Why?

- What did you enjoy about today? Why?

- What did you not enjoy about today? Why?

After a month, look back at what you wrote. The root cause of your problem—and where you should direct your energy—just may reveal itself.

Step 2: Evaluate Your Options

Once you identify the root cause of your problem, your next step is to find the most appropriate remedy. Should you fix the situation, live with the situation, or leave the situation? To find the right path, consider the following questions.

Has something you've experienced crossed the line?

Not every job or organization will allow for these things, but it's important to feel safe, to remain physically and mentally healthy, and to be able to be yourself. The more you feel that your situation at work is encroaching upon your safety, physical and mental health, or sense of self, the more serious and urgent your situation is—and the more empowered you should feel to fix the situation or leave the situation. And, of course, if you experience any sexism, racism, or any other "ism," know that you really do have a problem and deserve to have it addressed.

How local is your problem?

Think of your problem as a puddle that you're standing in. You could be standing in a small puddle, where the problem is confined to a certain set of people; a medium-size puddle, where your problem is confined to your place of employment; or a large puddle, where the problem is common to everyone in your type of role. Once you understand how big your puddle is, you'll know how far you need to step to get out (and how feasible it is to step out easily).

- If you have a *people* problem, ask yourself: *Would switching teams solve my problem? How feasible is this option?*

- If you have a *place* problem, ask yourself: *Would switching organizations solve my problem? How feasible is this option?*

- If you have a *position* problem, ask yourself: *Would switching professions solve my problem? How feasible is this option?*

But a warning: expect trade-offs. When I was a management consultant, my coworkers would often joke that projects came with good people, interesting work, or a good lifestyle. Some projects might offer two of the three, but many more would only offer one. It's no use holding out for a project that offers all three. Those don't exist. Figure 14-3 illustrates the tension.

FIGURE 14-3

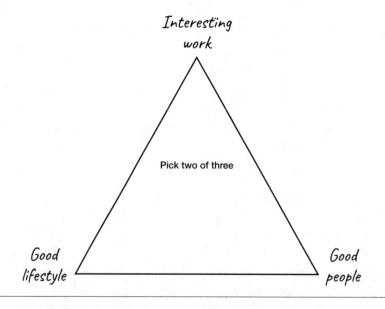

Trade-offs at work: An example

You could put other characteristics at the corners of this triangle, depending on your circumstances: high impact, good pay or benefits, low stress, good stability, good location. No matter what labels you put in your triangle, the conclusion is the same: no combination of people, position, and place will be perfect. It's a question of what you value and what you are willing to sacrifice.

If you are aren't sure what trade-offs you implicitly signed up for when you accepted your current role, look for patterns: Search for your employer and job type on Glassdoor, Reddit, YouTube, and blogs to see if others have reported issues similar to yours. If they have, you may have just uncovered a widespread or long-standing problem within your employer or profession that you'll need to decide if you can live with. You could also search for former employees of your organization on LinkedIn to see if there is a pattern of people switching roles or organizations after a year or less. If so, you may have uncovered a pattern of people not being able to live with or fix their problems. Don't forget to consult a trusted coworker or mentor in the organization to see if they share your concerns and, if so, how they've navigated the situation.

How temporary is your problem?

Difficult managers or coworkers may be frustrating, but they're less so if they are tied to a project that'll end in six months or if there's an option to transfer teams after a certain point. Bad work-life balance or low pay may be unsustainable, but they're less so if you know that your lifestyle will get better over time with seniority. Could Kathryn have requested a change in teams? We will never know—she never explored such an option.

Although the temporary nature of a problem doesn't make it any less painful or valid, it can change whether fixing, living with, or leaving your situation makes the most sense. If you think the long-term benefits of staying offset the short-term pain, then you may find fixing or living with the situation more appealing than leaving. If, on the other hand, you think the odds of getting to a better spot are slim, then leaving the situation may become a more compelling option. If nothing will change unless you incite a change, then the responsibility is yours—and yours alone.

What would a better situation look like?

Pretend that leaving is not an option and that you can change whatever you want about your situation. What would you change? What would your new setup look like? Whom would you need to convince to make this change? How reasonable a request would it be in the eyes of the decision makers?

In general, the more people you'd need to convince, the higher up they are, and the less reasonable they regard the change, the harder it will be to make it. The fewer people you'd need to convince, the lower down they are, and the more reasonable they deem your proposal, the easier your change should be to adopt.

If your problem is one that you can resolve with your manager—and if you haven't spoken to your manager about it yet—then you may want to consider the *fix it* option before the *leave it* or *live with it* options. If you're struggling to picture what a better setup would look like, consider reaching out to your network or searching online to see how other teams or organizations have handled a similar issue. It's likely that whoever you'll need to convince will ask, "So, what do you want me to do?" Give others something to react to. You will look much more credible and convincing if you can say, "This is the problem and this is my proposal" instead of "I don't know what I want; all I know is I don't like what I've been given."

What are the pros and cons of each option?

Consider drawing a two-column table like the one in table 14-1. In the left column, write down all of the reasons a certain option makes sense. In the right column, write out all the reasons it doesn't make sense.

As you list pros and cons, you will begin to see that some are more reasonable, acceptable, and convincing than others. Sometimes, it only takes a few pros and cons for you to decide that there really is an option that is superior to the others. There is also another benefit to this exercise: hopefully, it can help you see the positive in an otherwise difficult situation.

Keep in mind that your list of pros and cons can change depending on what you value, so consider checking in with yourself regularly, whether it's every month, three months, or six months. Are things looking better? If so, keep going. If not, reevaluate your options.

TABLE 14-1

Example pros and cons to consider when picking your resolution

Pros	Cons
Live with the situation	
✓ I can see the frustration ending by _____ .	✗ Life could be difficult for the next _____ .
✓ Makes me look like I'm cut out for the job, especially since no one else is complaining.	✗ If I don't speak up, the higher-ups may not even realize that there is a problem.
✓ I have more to learn. Maybe it isn't actually this bad once I learn how things work.	✗ My mental/physical health could suffer.
Fix the situation	
✓ Maybe people could see me as a leader for proposing solutions.	✗ I'm still new, so I might come across as entitled/demanding.
✓ If I leave later, at least I'll know I tried my best.	✗ Is this the one thing I want to ask for? What if something else comes up?
✓ I can see myself staying in this organization long-term, so I might as well try to make things better.	✗ I haven't been performing my best lately. Should I wait until I have more leverage?
Leave the situation	
✓ There is no long-term career path for me here.	✗ If I leave too soon/do this too frequently, I could look like a job hopper.
✓ I can probably maintain my professional relationships if I leave gracefully.	✗ Job searching will be a pain.
✓ I don't feel like I'm growing/learning here anymore.	✗ I haven't gotten everything I can out of this job yet.

Which option will I feel best about in ten minutes, ten months, and ten years?

Once you lay out your possible options, the last step is to do some time travel. Columnist Suzy Welch has what she calls the "10-10-10 strategy" for this.[1] Think multiple steps ahead: Which option feels most appealing ten minutes from now? Which might leave you more satisfied in ten months, after you experience the positive and negative consequences of your action (or inaction)? Which might leave you feeling the best in ten years, once you are many steps along in your career and have had the time to process all the trade-offs? The path of fastest relief or least effort may not be the same as the path of least regret. Time travel offers another benefit: it can help you take the emotion out of a decision. As Kathryn learned the hard way, when the pain is real and immediate, leaving the situation can feel like the best, or only, choice—when in reality, it may be nothing more than a quick but unsustainable fix.

Is your problem about others not being aware of their impact?

This can be a difficult possibility to embrace when the issue is fresh in your mind and emotions are high, but give it a chance. If the root cause of your problem is your manager or coworker, for example, could they not realize the consequences of their actions? (In Kathryn's case, might it be that her manager didn't realize that his management style wasn't working for her?) The higher the likelihood that others might say, "What? I had no idea!" the more you may want to consider fixing the situation before living with the problem or leaving it. If the root cause really does stem from the other person not realizing their negative impact, then the solution could be easier than you think. Sometimes, all it takes is a conversation.

Step 3: Fix the Problem Tactfully

When fixing your situation, the right approach can be the difference between getting what you want and making the situation worse. The unspoken rules we've covered elsewhere in this guide can help de-escalate conflicts: Think multiple steps ahead. Find the appropriate time and person. Correct privately. Push gently—but firmly. Make sure that your impact is positive. And treat the conversation as if you are trying to learn and help. You want to look like you are on the same team as the other person and trying to achieve a common goal, rather than demanding something where only you benefit. Here are some other strategies to consider when you're trying to fix something.

> **Don't go it alone. Ask for help.** Before approaching whomever you need to speak with, consider asking a trusted coworker to see if others have had similar issues before and, if so, how the

conversations went. Doing so can help you avoid making the same mistakes.

Don't criticize. Show appreciation. Consider overusing "Thanks . . . ," "I appreciate . . . ," and "I'm grateful for . . ." Positivity can be contagious and recognition can help make for a more cooperative atmosphere, so use them to set the right tone. Also, gratitude is free, so give it away.

Don't assume negative intent. Assume positive intent. Try saying, "I know you [have positive intent], so I suspect it wasn't your intent, but [negative impact]." Even if you don't actually think so, such a statement can help prevent others from getting defensive.

Don't talk about improving your life. Focus on contributing to the team. Instead of "I need _____," try saying, "I'd love to find a way for us to better _____." If anything you're suggesting can help the team, point it out. It makes you sound less demanding.

Don't point to problems. Ask for advice. Rather than say, "_____ is dumb," "_____ makes no sense," or "_____ is unsustainable," consider trying, "I'd love your advice on _____" or "How would you go about navigating _____?"

Don't propose changes. Offer experiments. People are more likely to embrace things that are low commitment. So, instead of saying, "We should change . . . ," consider saying, "I wonder if we could try . . . ," "Could we consider . . . ," or "We could experiment with . . ."

Don't dwell on the work. Look at the broader experience. If you have a people problem and those people are your teammates, you may want to expand your network. Try joining companywide events, affinity groups, and community service efforts. It's easier to shrug off a less-than-ideal situation if it's a single point of negativity within a broadly positive experience.

Here's how Kathryn could have applied these strategies to try to fix her situation:

Kathryn: "Any chance you might have thirty minutes at some point to catch up? I'd love to pick your brain on a few career-related questions."

Manager: "Sure! Go ahead and find a time. My calendar is up to date."

[Fast-forward to the conversation]

Kathryn: "Thanks for taking the time to meet. I know how busy you are, so I really appreciate you being so generous." [*Show appreciation*]

Manager: "My pleasure! Thanks for your hard work. I know it's not easy with this client."

Kathryn: "It's been great being a fly on the wall during these conference calls. This actually relates to what I was hoping to ask you about, which is how you went about finding your niche. I'm always impressed by how much knowledge you pull in from other domains and wanted to see how I could get myself to this level as a professional." [*Ask for advice*]

Manager: "It was all mentorship. I was lucky to have a number of mentors who pushed me to try new things. That's how I broke into both financial services and telecommunications. Not sure I'll do this forever, but I like it for now."

Kathryn: "That's helpful! I've also started exploring the telecommunications space recently and noticed that the team holds lunch-and-learns on Fridays and monthly happy hours. I've wanted to attend, but given the travel expectation with this client, it's been a challenge. I was wondering if you had any advice on how to navigate this situation." [*Ask for advice*]

Manager: "We can definitely work something out. Let me talk to the client and see if we can find some flexibility for you on Fridays."

People can't read your mind, so if you don't speak up, they may not even recognize that there's a problem. Had Kathryn had a conversation like this, she may not have had to resort to quitting.

Step 4: Leave Graciously

Sometimes your best attempt will still not be enough—and leaving is the only option left. How will you know if you've reached that point? Consider these ten questions:

- ☐ Have you tried living with (or working around) the issue?
- ☐ Have you asked allies for help?
- ☐ Have you identified what you want?
- ☐ Have you tried engaging with the individual?
- ☐ Have you tried escalating the issue?
- ☐ Have you tried switching teams?
- ☐ Have you exhausted the options you can think of?
- ☐ Have you reached the limits of your patience?
- ☐ Have you secured a suitable alternative job?
- ☐ Are you convinced that the alternative solves your problem?

You don't need to answer "yes" to all ten to leave, but the more questions you answer "yes" to, the more sense leaving makes. Another consideration is how long you've been in your role. In general, the unspoken rule is to try to stay in a job for at least a year (and ideally at least two years). There is also an unspoken rule about not jumping between companies too quickly, so you don't look like an uncommitted job hopper. This is not to say you can't or shouldn't leave, though. You can always exclude the experience from your résumé and find an external narrative for the employment gap.

Luckily, job transitions aren't only the result of people *running away* from something. You could also be *running toward* something, whether it's better people, a better position, or a better place. Whatever the reason— and no matter how desirable or undesirable that reason may be—it helps to leave your role as deliberately as you entered it. Here are five steps for gracefully navigating the exit:

Job hunt discreetly

If you know that your manager wants the best for you, even if it means helping you leave for another job, then feel free to share your plans early and often for their feedback. But if your manager is anything short of a loyal champion, then it's a good idea to be more discreet. This means making sure that your work attire doesn't look like you just came from a job interview—even if you did. It means using your personal email address and computer for job applications and correspondence with recruiters. It means keeping any job search–related calendar invitations off your work calendar. And it means making sure your LinkedIn profile doesn't show that you're looking for jobs. You want to signal unambiguous commitment to your managers, coworkers, and IT department until you are ready to share your plans (and, as we will soon discuss, until your very last day).

Make the announcement

A departing employee is always disruptive to a team. At the very least, your manager will need to hire someone to fill your role. And if you are the owner of any important projects or if a major deadline is approaching, your departure may be even more disruptive. The more you can minimize the disruption for others, the better the final impression you will leave. Although two weeks' notice is typical when announcing your resignation, try to give your manager as much advance notice as possible. I've given as much as two months' notice to provide my manager the time to prepare. Try to pick a departure date that is the least disruptive for your team, such as after a major deadline or when your team is less busy. Once you've identified a date or a range of options, set up a one-on-one meeting with your manager to share your plans. Announce your plans to your coworkers only after speaking with your manager. You don't want your manager finding out that you are leaving from anyone other than you.

Wind things down

Ask your manager what you can do to smooth the transition: Can you make enough progress on your current project that your successor can take over easily? Can you organize your files? Can you write a training manual or transition guide? Can you help find, interview, or train your replacement? The more you can present yourself as remaining committed to the team, even when you are on your way out, the better an impression you will leave behind—and the more likely your coworkers will want to work with you again.

Say your goodbyes

If you are working in person, consider buying some professional-looking thank-you cards and handwriting notes to each coworker, mentor, and ally. Be sure to tailor your message to the recipient. Here are a few starting points.

"Thank you for _____."

"It was great working with you on _____."

"I appreciate _____."

"I will always remember _____."

"I am grateful for _____."

If you work remotely and don't have people's mailing addresses, consider drafting personalized thank-you emails to send to each person on your last day. And whether you are working remotely or not, consider setting up one-on-one meetings with each close coworker, mentor, and ally to do one last catch-up session. On your last day, consider sending one last team email to everyone, and CC your personal email, as we will soon discuss.

This all might look like a lot of extra work, but the effort is worth it—even if you get laid off rather than quit. A CEO taught me this lesson through the story of his daughter, Joanna, who had been laid off from her startup job alongside a dozen other people as part of a companywide cost-cutting effort.

"I gave her one piece of advice," this CEO told me. "Pretend like this was the best thing that could have ever happened to you." He helped his daughter write a thank-you email to her colleagues. It looked something like this:

Subject: I'm cheering you all on!

Dear _____ family,

After two incredible years on the operations team, I'm afraid it's time to say goodbye. While I'm sad that I won't get to be a part of your next stage of growth, I cannot think of a better team to bring the vision of _____ to life.

Thank you for the friendship, mentorship, and opportunities you've provided to me during my time here. You welcomed a bright-eyed and bushy-tailed new grad into your ranks and showed her what it takes to be a world-class professional. A few specific shout-outs:

- Lushen, Catherine, and Kamau for your guidance and opportunity to help launch _____ to the Indian market

- Casey, Sonja, Ravi, and the go-to-market team for your great expertise, creativity, and infinite patience

- Samir, Carolina, Doug, and the leadership team for keeping us all rowing in the same direction and for creating a culture that I'm proud to have been a part of

Though my next steps are still unclear, my plan is to remain in San Francisco and to remain in the e-commerce space (let me know if you have any suggestions!).

Going forward, I can be reached at _____@_____.com and XXX-XXX-XXXX.

Gratefully yours,

Joanna

https://www.linkedin.com/in/_____

Joanna wasn't sure if she should send her email to the entire company, but decided to bend the rules and do it anyway. Several hours later, she received an email from the CEO of the company:

Subject: RE: I'm cheering you all on!

Joanna, what a class act!

What types of roles are you looking for? Let me dig through my network to see if I can make any introductions.

Joanna had made a positive impact—and a lasting impression. Looking back, this is what Joanna's dad told me: "People like to say that first impressions matter. Last impressions can matter just as much. It's such a low bar, too. When you announce that you're about to leave, most people assume that you'll be checked out. Anything you do that defies expectations and shows that you're still invested in the team can go a long way."

Stay in touch

Consider adding your coworkers on LinkedIn and, for the ones you were close to, using the tactics we discussed in chapter 11 to keep the relationship alive. Whoever you met in your job is now a part of your network. Nurture those relationships. Share relevant news. Be helpful. After all, your career will be long. Your first job will not be your last job. You never know where your colleagues may go—and how your paths might cross again.

Being unhappy at work isn't fun. At best, conflicts can be an annoying distraction. At worst, they can turn a good job into a nightmare. And because conflicts are fundamentally about people, even the seemingly minor ones can quickly lead to dread about going to work. I hope that you don't end up finding this chapter relevant. In the end, conflicts are a natural part of life. Knowing how to identify, prioritize, and deal with conflict is an important life skill. Now you have the tools to handle conflict—and not just to avoid it.

Try This

- Accept the fact that no job will be perfect and each job will have its limitations.

- When faced with a tough situation at work, try to find the root cause of the problem.

- Decide which option makes the most sense for you based on the pros and cons: live with the situation, fix the situation, or leave the situation.

- Find allies and push gently but firmly when approaching others about issues.

- If you leave, do so graciously, leaving behind the best last impression possible.

Show Your Potential

At this point in the guide, you may have started to wonder: *So, I know how to demonstrate my Three Cs—competence, commitment, and compatibility. Now what?*

This is where the biggest difference between school and work emerges. School is a conveyor belt: if you keep passing your classes, you keep moving forward. Work is a wilderness expedition: where you go and how quickly you get there is up to you—and the wilderness. These choices are now in your hands. Where do you want to go? Let's walk through some of your options, depending on what type of role you're in.

Internship, apprenticeship, part-time job, or contract role. You may decide that you want to either go somewhere else when the current opportunity ends or convert your current role into a full-time job.

Full-time role. You may decide that you want to keep doing what you are doing in your current role, get promoted to take on more-important responsibilities or move up the chain of command, switch to a different team, or leave the organization.

If you wish to get promoted, then it's time to prove yourself. This chapter is for you. And even if you wish to remain in your current role, consider reading this chapter anyway. Just because you want to stay in your

Know This

- You are evaluated based on both your performance (how effective you are in your current role) and your potential (how effective you can expect to be in your next role).

- Want to move up the chain of command, earn more responsibility, or secure a raise? Get ready to show both high performance and high potential.

role doesn't mean the universe will let you do it. Who knows: Your job could change, be outsourced, or be automated. Your organization could decide that it no longer needs your role to exist. The world could decide that it no longer needs your organization to exist. Before we dive into the steps to take to get promoted, let's figure out how and when people get promoted so you can get yourself into the right mindset.

How and When People Get Promoted

Most of this guide has been about proving yourself as an individual contributor (IC), a fancy term for someone who doesn't manage anyone. By pursuing a promotion, you are implicitly signing up to prove yourself again—at a higher level.

Why? Because when you first start out, you are at the bottom of the chain of command and so don't have anyone reporting to you. There is nowhere to move but up—and even if you remain an IC at the next level, the higher-ups will typically expect more of you. No longer can you simply do your job. You need to show your potential, not just your performance, as detailed in table 15-1. This will show people that you can go from executing to leading.

Now let's look at figure 15-1. The idea is to get as close as possible to the top-right corner of this chart, where high performance—how effective you are in your current role—and high potential—how effective you can expect to be in your next role—overlap. The closer you are to this corner, the more people recognize that you can perform well as an IC

TABLE 15-1

The difference between performance and potential

Performance	Potential
Can you do the current job well?	Can you do the next job well?
Are you excited to be here?	Are you excited to grow here?
Do you get along with us?	Can you lead us?

and have the potential to perform well as a leader. And the more people see both performance and potential from you, the higher your chances of getting promoted.

In some organizations (typically those with HR departments), this framework is called the "nine-box matrix" and is the backbone of the formal performance evaluation process. In these organizations, managers may score their subordinates after each project or each year, then submit the feedback to HR, which places everyone into one of the nine boxes. The process is repeated at every layer of the organization. During promotion or bonus time, a committee of higher-ups will use the matrix to decide whom to invest in. Some organizations even maintain secret lists of "high-potentials," people seen as future executives in the company. High-potentials may receive more opportunities for professional development, mentorship, or interesting assignments, including overseas rotations.

In organizations with less-structured HR processes, this matrix is unspoken, existing only in the minds of management—but it's still used to consider which employees to invest in and not. In general, the less structured an organization is with its promotion process, the more likely it is that your direct manager will decide whether you get a promotion—and the more important it becomes for the two of you to be compatible.

Some organizations, especially those outside white-collar work, take a different approach and look at qualifications (whether you have a certain license, for example) and seniority (how long you've worked in the organization). Because such roles and organizations resemble the "conveyor belt" of school, we will exclude them from our discussion.

Now that we've discussed *how* organizations decide to promote people, let's discuss *when* organizations decide to do it. Seniority-oriented

FIGURE 15-1

The nine-box matrix

Promotable   ↙ Be here! ☺

	Low performance	Medium performance	High performance
High potential	What's going on? Are you in the wrong job?	Wow! Let's develop you. Clearly you have what it takes.	Future leader! Let's give you more important responsibilities!
Medium potential	Let's see if we can coach you so you get better.	You're a solid teammate. Let's continue to see how well you do.	You're awesome! Let's keep challenging you.
Low potential	You can't do your current job and likely can't do your next job. Fire!	Let's keep giving you do-as-I-say tasks.	Let's keep you in your current job and maybe have you train others.

Not here! ↗
☹

organizations aside, promotions typically happen under three circumstances: every few years (in "up or out" organizations), when there is a vacancy, or when there is a new need in the organization. Figure 15-2 lays out these three circumstances.

"Up or out" is a fancy way of saying that you need to be promoted within a certain time frame or else look for another job. It is seen in some investment banking, consulting, or accounting firms that are large enough and have enough turnover (employees leaving) to promote people on a somewhat regular basis. To get promoted in "up or out" environments, you will typically need to stay at or near the top-right corner relative to your peers and show improvement over time.

In organizations where people stay a while, you may need to wait for a job vacancy (opening) to emerge when someone above you moves to a different role, quits, gets fired, or retires. In these cases, rising up isn't the default option; staying in your current role is. To be selected

FIGURE 15-2

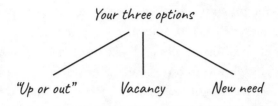

When you can expect to get promoted

Your three options

"Up or out"   Vacancy   New need

when a position opens, you need to be seen as high-performance and high-potential long before an opportunity arises.

If you work at in small organization or startup, then there may be even less opportunity for you to get promoted. If the organization is just you and the founding team, for example, then there may not be an obvious next step up, let alone a structured performance evaluation process. Instead, promotions happen because there's a "business case" for it—because management is convinced that promoting you will help the organization achieve its goals.

Although the process may look different depending on where you work, the theory is similar: a promotion is an investment—in you. And like all investments, people want to be sure it will have a high chance of paying off before they contribute their time, money, and energy.

What does this mean for you? Let's dive in!

How to Position Yourself for a Promotion

The key to getting promoted is to find an unoccupied swimlane that matters to your team—and then claim it. How do you find one? Ask yourself five questions.

What can I do that hasn't been done?

Most organizations value the same four things: more customers, clients, donors, and fans; better products, services, and reviews; faster ways of getting things done; and cheaper ways to keep everything running. If you can achieve one or more of these goals, you can boost others' perceptions of your potential—and your promotability.

This was the strategy that Ketty took to transform her temporary office assistant role into a full-time marketing coordinator position, a role that had never existed before. Her company made money by finding nurses who were looking for jobs and matching them with open hospital positions. Ketty's job was to process all of the nurses' paperwork. While doing her job, Ketty recognized a pattern: the higher-ups kept complaining that, although hospitals always wanted to hire more nurses, somehow her company was never able to find enough candidates.

Duh! Ketty thought as she listened to the executives. *You are relying on emails and phone calls to recruit nurses when all of my nursing friends are using social media to find their jobs. No wonder you aren't finding enough people!* Ketty used her social media apps to search for the keywords "nurse" and "jobs." She found dozens of groups containing tens of thousands of nurses who were sharing career advice. Ketty took screenshots of all the groups she found, then compiled a list of links for her supervisor. Then she emailed her supervisor a plan to post open jobs in these groups.

Her supervisor forwarded the email up the chain of command. Her supervisor's own manager loved the idea and suggested that Ketty help execute the plan. Ketty did, and also created a social media page for the company. Within several weeks, the firm had attracted thousands of followers and likes.

Four months into Ketty's six-month contract, her supervisor approached her. "I hope you aren't going anywhere. We want you here full time." Ketty turned her dead-end temp role into a full-time offer for a marketing job she was excited about—and then later became one of the youngest managers in the company. How did she do it? By helping her company recruit more candidates with a method that was both faster and cheaper than before. Ketty got promoted not because the higher-ups had planned to do it, but because they saw the benefits of keeping her—and investing in her.

If you're ever using your team's usual methods of getting work done and find yourself thinking, *Man, this is so outdated* or *Why aren't we doing* _____ *instead?* consider writing down your idea and bringing it up once you've done your have-to-do tasks fully and correctly. But be mindful of two things.

First, try to focus on methods that are *better* and not simply different. Your idea needs to improve the current situation; it can't just be your own way of doing things. You are proposing a change to the usual process—and change can be not only uncomfortable but also potentially threatening to supporters of the old way. The more you can convince others that the pros of your way outweigh the pros of the old way, the more likely people will listen to you. Use your influencer networks to your advantage. They can help you understand what's been tried, what's failed, and which allies you might need on your side.

Second, know that some flavors of *more, better, faster,* and *cheaper* can be more important—and promotable—than others. From the perspective of the higher-ups, changes can be noticed or not noticed and reported or not reported. In Ketty's case, introducing a better way to recruit people likely would have been noticed by the higher-ups. But an increase in, for example, how often the communal fridge is cleaned likely wouldn't have been reported to them. This again speaks to the unfortunate reality of office housework.

If you have multiple ideas, consider ranking them from most noticed and most reported to least noticed and least reported, as seen in figure 15-3. Consider also what's urgent and important for your team and

FIGURE 15-3

Types of changes to focus on to get promoted

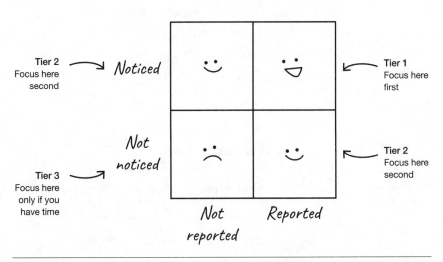

organization. The more urgent and important your idea is for helping the team achieve its goals, the more likely it will be noticed and reported. But remember: just because a task is neither noticed nor reported to the higher-ups doesn't mean it isn't important. When you are new or junior, embracing tasks that aren't always noticed or reported is how you build trust, establish yourself as a team player, and prove that you aren't entitled. (That's why this chapter is near the end of the book.)

What can I fix that hasn't been fixed?

Problems in the workplace sit on a spectrum. On one end are minor itches (inconveniences that people are willing to live with). On the other end are mission-critical problems (issues that could derail a project—or maybe even the organization—if not resolved). Somewhere in the middle, but still close to the mission-critical side, are massive pains (issues that waste a lot of time, especially for higher-ups, or cause a lot of stress). The more you align yourself with solving massive pains and mission-critical problems, the more likely people will be to recognize your potential—and your promotability. (See figure 15-4.) To identify these massive pains and mission-critical problems, pay attention to how often your manager and other higher-ups complain about something. The higher up the complainers are, the more complainers there are, and the more they complain, the bigger the opportunity may be. The better you understand what matters to those who matter, the better your odds of making an impact—and the better your chances of getting promoted.

Here's an example. Imane, a software engineer at a tech company, noticed that her team was releasing product features randomly, rather than on a schedule. As a result, customers were getting confused, man-

FIGURE 15-4

Types of problems to focus on to get promoted

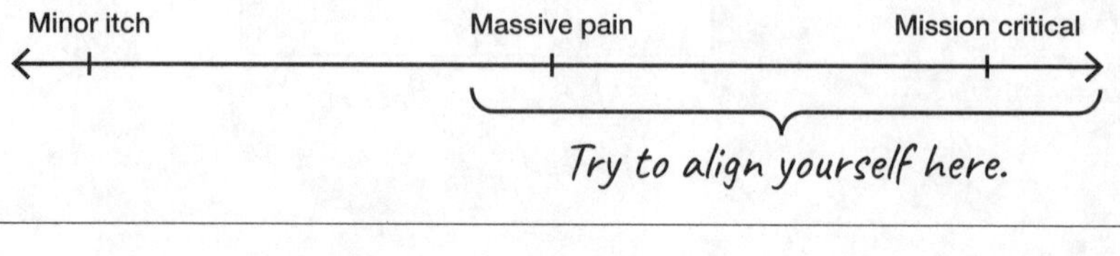

Minor itch   Massive pain   Mission critical

Try to align yourself here.

agers were getting blindsided, and teams were doing overlapping work. Imane went to the person responsible for releasing features and asked, "Do we have a software release schedule of some sort?" When her co-worker shrugged, Imane asked, "Would it be helpful if I put a schedule together?" The coworker agreed. Imane then met with each teammate to hear their ideas. She put together a plan, sought feedback from her teammates, secured her coworkers' and manager's approvals, and then launched her idea at an all-hands meeting. Thanks to Imane's idea, the team followed a structured process for releasing all future product features, and she ended up being praised for her leadership in her year-end review. Later on, Imane was promoted to senior software engineer sooner than her peers. And it all began with her fixing what hadn't been fixed.

Of course, as we have learned throughout this book, what you do is only half the battle. How you do it without being threatening can be just as important. So, before proposing solutions, consider consulting a coworker who's close to the problem to learn why things are the way they are. If someone's not doing their job, be wary of overstepping. If ambition is your intent, then you risk aggression becoming your impact—unless you carefully navigate how to bring your ideas forward.

This is true for all unoccupied swimlanes. You can't—and won't—make everyone happy. Try your best, but don't beat yourself up if not everyone is on your side. Remember: Problems at work aren't monsters to run away from. They're opportunities to run toward. It's within problems that opportunities are created, trust is built, and careers are made.

What can I bridge that hasn't been bridged?

You don't always need to come up with something new or fix some massive problem to be noticed. Sometimes, all you need to do is be a "bridge" between people, between topics, or between people and topics.

Translators are people who can speak the "language" of two domains, cultures, or ways of thinking—and who can turn one side's jargon and ideas into terms that the other side can understand. Some people are literally translators. One intern I spoke to at a pharmaceutical company was invited to important client meetings because she was the only person on the team who could speak Spanish. A salesperson at a tech company, on the other hand, was able to translate his sales team's rambling thoughts into simple charts, graphs, and slides that won the approval of the data-minded people on the marketing team.

Facilitators are people who help others get along. They step in and serve as neutral go-betweens, introducing people to each other or helping both sides resolve conflicts. A career adviser I met became friendly with administrators across different schools at his university, and so was invited to—and had a say in—almost every meeting between departments.

Combiners are people who can use two domains to create something better than either domain could produce alone. An academic researcher combined his love of podcasts with his professional work to help his research institute launch and market a podcast, for example. A volunteer for an educational program used his graphic design skills to transform the program's boring documents into fun infographics.

The key to playing any of these bridge roles—or even all of them at the same time—is to give yourself credit for what and who you know. If you ever find yourself thinking, *I understand both* _____ *and* _____. *Why is it so hard for everyone else?* you may have found a hidden opportunity to be a translator. If you ever find yourself thinking, *I get along with* _____ *and* _____ *just fine. Why aren't they communicating?* you may have found a hidden opportunity to be a facilitator. If you find yourself thinking, _____ *could really learn a thing or two from the world of* _____, then you may have found a hidden opportunity to be a combiner. No one thinks exactly like you do, so if you see a way to connect the dots that others don't, show them.

What can I know that others don't know?

A finance analyst attended a company training where she learned how to use some new data analytics software. She returned to her team—where everyone was still using spreadsheets—and magically did her work in a fraction of the time. Overnight, she became the team's *tool* expert.

Another time, the CEO of one startup called the COO of a different startup and asked, "Hey, I heard you've worked with this venture capital firm before. What are they like?" In the eyes of the CEO, the COO was a *person* expert.

An international development consultant in Japan wanted to work in Southeast Asia for his company, but never got picked because he didn't have any experience in the region. He took a leave of absence, interned for a social enterprise in Myanmar, and, during his leave, cold emailed senior members of his company to share what he had been working on and how his work was relevant to the company. By the time he returned to his old job, he not only got pulled into multiple Southeast Asia projects but also became an internal expert on the region. Within three months, he became a *topic* expert.

If you suffer from impostor syndrome—meaning you tend to doubt your abilities and doubt that you belong in your job—it can be difficult to consider yourself an expert at anything. In teams with more-experienced, faster-thinking, and louder-talking coworkers, it can be especially easy to tell yourself, *Everyone is so smart here! How could I ever have anything useful to say?* or *I'm no expert—I just heard this information from someone else.* If you've ever found yourself thinking these thoughts, you may have set your standards too high. You don't need to be the world's foremost expert on a tool, person, or topic to be valuable as a local expert on your team. You only need to know slightly more than your teammates.

Just one caveat: although becoming a tool expert can be powerful because new tools give you an edge in achieving better, faster, or cheaper, it's important to be careful. If you're the only one who knows how to use a certain tool, it can be easy for others to become reliant on you. So, if you don't want to be assigned a certain task all the time, be careful to not come across as *too* competent. Be an expert, but only in the things you truly want to be an expert in.

What can I share that hasn't been shared?

Don't discount what you come across, learn, or create in your everyday work and personal life. You may have something that could be valuable to and worth sharing with your coworkers. That "something" can often come in two flavors: templates (anything you've created that others can reuse or adapt) and information (any news, data, or observations that may be relevant to others' work or interests).

A manager at a logistics company once told me about a member of her team who created lots of Excel templates in his job. After each project, he'd ask his manager, "I made these models [spreadsheets] and would hate to have them go to waste. Would it be OK if I uploaded them to the company intranet for others?" After getting permission, he removed confidential information from his models, added cover pages explaining how each file worked, inserted comment boxes throughout describing each feature, and then uploaded them under his and his team's name. In sharing the files, this individual subtly signaled not only his desire to help and be a team player but also that he was a tools and topic expert, a reputation that led to others coming to him for guidance.

"I kept getting complimented out of nowhere," this person's manager told me. "People were like, 'Oh man, you guys saved us!' We earned so many favors from other teams."

Any time you create or learn about something, consider asking yourself, "Could this be useful to others?" "Is this OK to share beyond those involved?" and "Would my manager be OK with it?" If the answer is "yes" to all three questions, consider sharing it.

Though being generous is important, as with all the unspoken rules in this guide, it's important to mirror others and follow the usual process. A communications associate once told me that many of her teammates would send "wins of the quarter" emails praising the team, while subtly showcasing what they did themselves. On that team, if you only praised yourself, you could be seen as overbearing and incompatible. If you only praised other people, you would miss the chance to signal your competence and commitment.

Another option—perhaps an even easier one—is to simply keep your eyes open for any news, reports, announcements, videos, or even podcast episodes that might be relevant to your coworkers. As we discussed in chapter 11, sending relevant information can not only sustain the momentum in a relationship but also signal to others that you are always on top of the latest developments.

If you want it, ask for it

So far, we've approached promotions as if your performance and potential will be recognized naturally. That may be true in some cases, but in others you may need to ask for what you want—and deserve. This was what happened with Galina, a program director at a large public university. After two and a half years in her job, Galina had launched and grown her university's public service program to be the largest in the university system. She had taken on a completely new and expanded role within the university—but hadn't seen a title change or salary increase. So, she decided to renegotiate her salary. First, she texted several of her friends who worked in similar roles at peer universities:

> Hey Aba, please excuse the personal question, but would you mind sharing your salary with me? I'm thinking of negotiating my salary and wanted to ask around for some comparison data points. In exchange, I'll share my findings with you!

Galina was shocked by what she learned: she had the lowest salary of all her peers despite running a larger program and having more education. She created a one-page comparison table showing her colleagues' institutions, salaries, education levels, years of experience, number of students served, and program offerings. She calculated the median salary, highlighted the peer who most closely resembled her in role and background, and decided to ask her manager for similar compensation. After two weeks of practicing her pitch, Galina approached her department head after a meeting.

"By the way," Galina started, "I'd like to have a conversation with you about my role. Do you have time in the coming days to chat?"

At their meeting, Galina explained her situation: "Thanks for taking the time to chat. I really appreciate it. I have loved working with you and love this team and am excited about all the new initiatives we are launching this year. I wanted to chat because it occurred to me recently that while my portfolio of responsibilities has doubled over the last two to three years, my salary hasn't increased."

Galina then pulled out her comparison table. "I made this table comparing my peers at other schools within our university system. As you can see, I launched and now run a program that is about twice as large as the programs at our peer institutions. I also have a master's degree, which several of my peers do not. But when I look at my salary, I am well below the level my peers are at. I would like to achieve pay equity with my peers, which would be 14 percent more than where I am at today. It would mean a lot to me to have your support to advocate for this increase. Would that be possible?"

The department head looked at Galina's one-pager—and then smiled. "Wow. I don't think I've ever seen such an organized document before. All the other times people just said, 'I want more money' without giving me anything tangible to help me advocate for them. Let me talk to my supervisor."

Two months later, Galina's manager returned with an update. She would receive a salary increase in the next fiscal year.

This didn't end up being Galina's last time asking for a raise. Two years later, she asked to participate in a professional development program that would cost $5,000 in fees, travel, and accommodations. And when she was denied another raise several years later, she applied for—and successfully secured—a higher-paying job at a peer institution. When she showed her department head the job offer, he immediately contacted HR, which offered to match the salary.

Looking back, Galina told me:

> *It was really hard for me to convince myself to negotiate my salary. I felt like I should be grateful for what I had because I was already making more money than anyone in my immediate family as a first-generation college student and immigrant . . . I felt guilty asking for more . . . I had to tell myself that this wasn't about the money; it was about valuing my self-worth, which was not reflected in my salary . . . I was working nights and weekends and wasn't being valued for my time . . . You have to ask. And if they say "no," see if there are other things you can get, like an increase to your professional development budget.*

Not everyone will know that you are being undervalued. Not everyone will know that you are going above and beyond. And no one will care more about your career than you. You obviously shouldn't ask for a promotion if you are still climbing your way to the top-right corner of the performance and potential matrix. But if you are already dominating that spot and still aren't being recognized for it, it might be time to seek the recognition yourself. Consider using the strategies we've discussed throughout this guide: When in doubt, consider asking a coworker you trust about the usual process. Know your audience. Do your homework. Think multiple steps ahead to picture how the conversation will go.

When you show up, save others time and stress by offering something for them to react to. And push gently but firmly.

Being valued begins with you. If you don't value yourself, others won't, either.

You Won't Always Get What You Want

As much as we'd like to think that all hard work and talent will be recognized and rewarded, unfortunately, the world isn't always fair. Sometimes, you may set yourself up for a promotion and not get it because of a lack of objectivity or a lack of opportunity.

A lack of objectivity

Don't let the authoritative-looking boxes in the nine-box matrix fool you into thinking that landing a promotion is a mechanical process, like putting money into a vending machine. It's not a machine that makes the decision; it's humans. Unfortunately, by now we already know where this people business leads: bias. Here's just one example: managers tend to use more-positive words (e.g. "analytical," "dependable," and "confident") to describe men in performance evaluations and more-negative words (e.g., "selfish," "passive," and "indecisive") to describe women.[1] It's not a level playing field.

Some organizations do a better job than others at addressing bias. Some have "360-degree feedback" processes where evaluations will be sought from not only an individual's manager but also from everyone who works with the individual. Other organizations establish promotion committees of higher-ups who do not know candidates personally and review employee records that have been stripped of any clues to an individual's gender or race. Typically, however, these are processes only larger organizations have. The smaller the organization, the more likely promotions will be based on people's gut feel about your Three Cs. And the smaller the organization, the more likely that your manager will be the one who decides on your promotion—and the more your future in the organization will hinge on your compatibility with this individual.

Depending on your circumstances, this can be good or bad. Some managers will prioritize what's best for *you*. Others will prioritize what's best for *them*. Sometimes you may have a manager who feels threatened by you or simply doesn't like you. Some managers think, *Well, if I didn't get my promotion, you shouldn't get yours, either.* You may already know from your manager's patterns of behavior what type of boss you have. And if you don't, you will—the topic of promotions has a way of revealing people's true colors. If—despite your best efforts to maximize your competence, commitment, and compatibility—your manager is still a hindrance, then it may be time to evaluate whether you could get further faster working for someone else.

A lack of opportunity

Just because you do a good job doesn't mean you will be successful in the organization. It also doesn't mean the organization will be successful. In startups, small nonprofits, or politics, for example, you may be the most talented person ever but still struggle to get promoted, not because of your underperformance or lack of potential, but because of your circumstances. Say you worked in sales at a startup that makes anchovy-flavored toothpaste. You could be an amazing salesperson but not sell much toothpaste—because no one wants that flavor. And if you have the misfortune of working for delusional higher-ups, *their* incompetence (in making bad product decisions) could be misinterpreted as *your* incompetence (in not being able to sell the product). And even if your supernatural skills do somehow lead to sales, the company still might not have enough resources to give you a promotion.

Even if you aren't at an organization that makes a bad product, you can experience a lack of opportunity. If you are working remotely, you may miss out on chances to observe higher-ups and coworkers and to identify unoccupied swimlanes. In these cases, you may need to pay extra-close attention in team meetings and be especially engaged with your coworkers on instant messenger to know what others are working on. You may also need to proactively propose ideas to your manager, rather than wait for assignments to be handed to you.

And then there are factors beyond your specific job. Maybe it's a bad economy. Maybe the industry is doing poorly. Maybe your department is getting restructured or your supportive manager left for another role. Whatever the reason, you could do a great job and still not get ahead.

Although it never hurts to build a reputation as someone who exceeds expectations, feeling stuck can be frustrating—and may mean it's time to look toward the next chapter of your career.

In the end, showing your potential is about convincing others that an investment in you is an investment that's good for the organization. It's about proving that you are not merely good at your job, but indispensable to the team. You may not be able to control the wind and snow on this wilderness expedition that is your career, but at least you will have done all that you can to set yourself up for success—and paved a path of least regret for yourself.

Try This

- Aim to demonstrate both high performance and high potential.

- Think beyond your specific job or swimlane to the broader goals of the organization.

- Ask yourself, "What can I do that hasn't been done?"; "What can I fix that hasn't been fixed?"; "What can I bridge that hasn't been bridged?"; "What can I know that others don't know?"; and "What can I share that hasn't been shared?"

- If you aren't getting recognized, seek out the recognition yourself.

AFTERWORD

In chapter 15, we compared your career to a wilderness expedition. We discussed that where you go and how quickly you get there is up to you—and the wilderness—to negotiate. That analogy isn't quite right.

Hiking up a mountain is a negotiation between humans and nature. Hiking up a career is a negotiation between humans and humans. A good map may get you far if you are hiking up a mountain, but it isn't enough if you are hiking up a career. Mountains may be hiked alone; careers cannot. To hike a career, you need more than just a map. You need someone to pull you up.

You need a good boss. And a good boss's boss. And a good boss's boss's boss—all the way to the top. Career success is a two-way street (or, in this case, trail). You need to have the desire to reach your full potential, but your boss—and every boss above them—also needs to create the conditions for everyone—not just the few—to reach their full potential. They need to train you, coach you, celebrate you, value you, be fair to you, and, when you fumble, forgive you.

Unfortunately, not everyone receives such treatment. Whether it's bias or unrealistic expectations, not all managers pull everyone up—and not all organizations lift everyone up. It is in these situations that we reach the limits of individual effort and enter the territory of the collective struggle—the struggle of paying it forward. We all have a role to play. *You* have a role to play.

Go ahead and use these unspoken rules to navigate your way to career success. But as you move forward, don't forget about those who remain behind. Answer that cold email. Mentor that stranger. Help that outsider. Support that coworker. Share that knowledge. Then, when you find yourself becoming someone else's boss, become the boss that you wish you could have had. Withhold that judgment. Hire that unproven candidate. Develop that employee. Offer that pep talk. Share that opportunity. Reward that hard work. Fight that injustice.

Use whatever opportunity you have to build a more fair and just workplace—and world. Pay it forward, as the more than five hundred professionals who've contributed to this guide have done for you.

Pass on the rules that make people work better together. Abolish the rules that don't give others a chance. With any luck, the next generation of early-career professionals won't even need this guide, because every one of them will have an equal opportunity to succeed, thanks to you and others like you.

The book may be over, but your career is just beginning. Visit gorick .com for more resources. Now go forward—and make an impact!

NOTES

Chapter 1

1. Lauren A. Rivera, "Hiring as Cultural Matching: The Case of Elite Professional Service Firms," *American Sociological Review* 77, no. 6 (2012): 999–1022; Miller McPherson, Lynn Smith-Lovin, and James M. Cook, "Birds of a Feather: Homophily in Social Networks," *Annual Review of Sociology* 27 (2001): 415–444; Emilio J. Castilla and Stephen Benard, "The Paradox of Meritocracy in Organizations," *Administrative Science Quarterly* 55 (2010): 543–576.

2. Dongwon Oh, Eldar Shafir, and Alexander Todorov, "Economic Status Cues from Clothes Affect Perceived Competence from Faces," *Nature Human Behaviour* 4 (2020): 287–293; Erez Levon et al., *Accent Bias: Implications for Professional Recruiting* (Accent Bias in Britain, 2020), https://accentbiasbritain.org/wp-content/uploads/2020/03/Accent-Bias-Britain -Report-2020.pdf; Lauren A. Rivera, *Pedigree: How Elite Students Get Elite Jobs* (Princeton: Princeton University Press, 2016); Jens Agerström and Dan-Olof Rooth, "The Role of Automatic Obesity Stereotypes in Real Hiring Discrimination," *Journal of Applied Psychology* 96, no. 4 (2011): 790–805.

3. Joan C. Williams and Rachel Dempsey, *What Works for Women at Work: Four Patterns Working Women Need to Know* (New York: NYU Press, 2018); Costas Cavounidis and Kevin Lang, "Discrimination and Worker Evaluation," NBER working paper no. 21612, National Bureau of Economic Research, Cambridge, MA, October 2015; Simon M. Laham, Peter Koval, and Adam L. Alter, "The Name-Pronunciation Effect: Why People Like Mr. Smith More Than Mr. Colquhoun," *Journal of Experimental Social Psychology* 48, no. 3 (2012), 752–756.

Chapter 5

1. Sam Friedman and Daniel Laurison, *The Class Ceiling: Why It Pays to Be Privileged* (Bristol, United Kingdom: Policy Press, 2019).

Chapter 7

1. Edward T. Hall, *The Silent Language* (New York: Doubleday & Company, 1959).

Chapter 9

1. Dwight D. Eisenhower, "Address at the Second Assembly of the World Council of Churches, Evanston, Illinois," speech, August 19, 1954, https://web.archive.org/web/20150402111315/http://www.presidency.ucsb.edu/ws/?pid=9991.

2. Linda Babcock et al., "Gender Differences in Accepting and Receiving Requests for Tasks with Low Promotability," *American Economic Review* 107, no. 3 (2017): 714–747.

3. Vanessa Fuhrmans, "Where Are All the Women CEOs?," *Wall Street Journal*, February 6, 2020, https://www.wsj.com/articles/why-so-few-ceos-are-women-you-can-have-a-seat-at-the-table-and-not-be-a-player-11581003276.

4. Rosabeth Moss Kanter, *Men and Women of the Corporation*, 2nd ed. (New York: Basic Books, 1993).

5. Joan C. William et al., *Climate Control: Gender and Racial Bias in Engineering?* (Center for WorkLife Law, UC Hastings College of the Law, 2016), https://worklifelaw.org/publications/Climate-Control-Gender-And-Racial-Bias-In-Engineering.pdf.

6. Madeline E. Heilman and Julie J. Chen, "Same Behavior, Different Consequences: Reactions to Men's and Women's Altruistic Citizenship Behavior," *Journal of Applied Psychology* 90, no. 3 (2005): 431–441.

7. Babcock et al., "Gender Differences in Accepting and Receiving Requests for Tasks with Low Promotability."

Chapter 11

1. John M. Gottman and Joan DeClaire, *The Relationship Cure: A Five-Step Guide to Strengthening Your Marriage, Family, and Friendships* (New York: Three Rivers Press, 2002).

Chapter 13

1. Erin Meyer, *The Culture Map: Breaking Through the Invisible Boundaries of Global Business* (New York: PublicAffairs, 2014).

2. Edward T. Hall, *The Silent Language* (New York: Doubleday & Company, 1959).

3. Thomas J. DeLong, "Three Questions for Effective Feedback," hbr.org, August 4, 2011, https://hbr.org/2011/08/three-questions-for-effective-feedback.

Chapter 14

1. Suzy Welch, *10-10-10: A Life-Transforming Idea* (New York: Simon & Schuster, 2009).

Chapter 15

1. David G. Smith et al., "The Power of Language: Gender, Status, and Agency in Performance Evaluations," *Sex Roles* 80 (2019): 159–171.

INDEX

ACKNOWLEDGMENTS

This baby has many parents. Over nine hundred, actually. It is the effort of the following individuals—and any others I am bound to have forgotten—that made this project possible. These are the people who've mentored me, opened doors for me, helped me uncover my blind spots, endured my countless rounds of questioning, offered shoulders to cry on, and helped me transform my napkin notes and shower thoughts into dozens of drafts—and, finally, into the book now in your hands. If you found it helpful, know that it didn't come just from me; it came from an entire village.

When I was a wide-eyed MBA student, Professor Len Schlesinger answered my cold email in six minutes and, just as quickly during our first meeting, encouraged me to turn my research into a book. Len readily embraced my ambitious independent project proposal, reviewed my early drafts, walked me through the unspoken rules of publishing, and introduced me to Paul B. Brown, who opened the door to my first publisher pitch. Although the pitch, like the nineteen that followed it, ended in rejection, I am grateful for—and learned a great deal from—the opportunity.

Jaime B. Goldstein, my startup pitch competition judge turned manager turned mentor turned friend, taught me that good is better than perfect (a lesson I am still trying to learn) and encouraged me to put myself out there, even though I didn't feel ready. She introduced me to Scott Belsky, who in turn introduced me to Jim Levine, my literary agent.

Jim Levine not only saw potential in my concept, but was, along with Matthew Huff and Courtney Paganelli, a constant source of encouragement in the face of rejection. Jim also taught me what has since become one of my favorite lines: "You only need one yes."

For being an unrelenting source of support during all the ups and downs, I thank "The Choir": Michael Altman, Camille Zumwalt Coppola, Eric Hendey, Lea Hendey, Vishnu Kalugotla, Ken Liu, and Chaodan Zheng.

For being a constant source of guidance, inspiration, and friendship as a fellow first-gen on a mission to level the playing field for those from humble beginnings, I thank David Carey—and Shawn Bohen for bringing us together.

For enduring my endless questions, reading—and rereading—my countless drafts, shaping my thinking and writing, and telling me what I *need* to hear rather than what I *want* to hear, I thank the brain trust that includes Aaron Altabet, Damaris Altomerianos, Kweku Darteh Anane-Appiah, Isaiah Baldissera, Julia Canick, Wadnes Castelly, Jim Chan, Chris Cheng, Joanna Cornell, Evan Covington, Caroline Davis, Matthew De La Fuente, Eugenio Donati, Neel Doshi, Sheila Enamandram, Uriel Epstein, Rebecca Feickert, Triston Francis, Collin Fu, Galina Gheihman, Luke Hodges, Winston Huang, Samir Junnarkar, Victor Kamenker, Joyce Kim, Leo Kim, Kieren Kresevic Salazar, Ling Lam, Alison Lee, Angela Li, Christian Lin, Jarron Lord, Monica MacGillis, Kamau Massey, Sana Mohammed, Miranda Morrison, Hasib Muhammad, Injil Muhammad Jr., Veronica O'Brien, Richard Park, Wes Peacock, Jan Philip Petershagen, Sudheer Poluru, Michele Popadich, Kathleen Power, Rachel Pregun, Josh Roth, Caleb Schwartz, Stephen Slater, Donovan Smith, Rob Snyder, Scott Stirrett, Meghan Titzer, George Vinton, Davis Wilkinson, Charles Wong, and Lushen Wu.

For their cheerleading and thought partnership during the manuscript's early stages, I thank the founding fellows of the Harvard Initiative for Learning and Teaching: Mahdi AlBasri, Sophie Turnbull Bosmeny, Azeez Gupta, Angela Jackson, and Susan Johnson McCabe.

For doing nothing short of magic with a manuscript that was forty thousand words over the word limit, I thank Alicyn Zall, my editor. I also thank Sally Ashworth, Julie Devoll, Lindsey Dietrich, Stephani Finks, Brian Galvin, Erika Heilman, Jeff Kehoe, Alexandra Kephart, Melinda Merino, Ella Morris, Josh Olejarz, Jon Shipley, Felicia Sinusas, Anne Starr, and everyone on the Harvard Business Review Press editorial, production, and commercial teams for transforming a Word document and a collection of hand-drawn sketches into a finished book.

For helping me start my career off right—and for being the intellectual and practical foundation of this project—I thank members of the BCG and BCG Digital Ventures family: Hachem Alaoui Soce, Spenta Arnold, Lia Asquini, Ben Aylor, Mohammed Badi, Simon Bartletta, Robert Batten, William Blonna, Adrienne Bross, William Brown, Jamie Brush, Keith Caldwell, Joe Carrubba, Rajiv Chegu, Caitlin Wolff Clifford, Peter Czerepak, Carl Daher, David DeSandre, Alexander Drummond, Meaghan English, Sheila Flynn, James Foley, Leah Fotis, Jared Ganis, Priya Garg, Anika Gupta, Michael Haghkerdar, Gary Hall, Daniel Harvey, Justine Hasson, Bryan Head, Jeri Herman, Max Horsley, Daniel Huss, Harnish Jani, Khatchig Karamanoukian, Scott Keenan, Rhanhee Stella Kim, Vladimir Kirichenko, Akifumi Kita, Allison Koo, Amit Kumar, Olga LaBelle, Hana Lane, Cici Liu, Elizabeth Lyle, Nate MacKenzie, Justin McBride, Eric Michel, Sara Schwartz Mohan, Emily Mulcahy, Scott Myslinski, Cara Nealon, Hikmat Noujeim, Chrissy O'Brien, Sarah Olsen, Richard Pierre, Roger Premo, Chloe Qi, Marisa Rackson, Sruthi Ravi, Roman Regelman, Eduardo Daniel Russian, Tom Schnitzer, Dorian Simpson, Aishwarya Sridhar, Chetan Tadvalkar, Jordan Taylor, Nithya Vaduganathan, Orian Welling, Ryah Whalen, John Wu, Graham Wyatt, Wenjia (Grace) You, Bill Young, Luke H. Young, Josh Zeidman, Jeff Zhang, and Kuba Zielinski.

For helping to demystify the unspoken rules of publishing, I thank Becky Cooper, Franklin Sooho Lee, Efosa Ojomo, Aemilia Phillips, Martin Roll, and Julie Zhuo.

For being thought partners and cheerleaders since the very beginning of this journey—and for staying with me despite my many flavors du jour—I thank Ethan Barhydt, Sam Barrows, Omnia Chen, Shuo Chen, Rob Cherun, Shao Yuan Chew Chia, Isabella Chiu, Dianne Ciarletta, Joshua Caleb Collins, Stephanie Connaughton, Eric Dallin, Zachary Dearing, Varun Desai, Kelly Graham, Laura Hogikyan, Marcel Horbach, Nathaniel Houghton, Sherjan Husainie, Mohammad Hanif Jhaveri, Jaxson Khan, Sherman Lam, Jenny Le, DI Lee, Dustin Leszcynski, Ketty Lie, Tianyu Liu, Justin Lo, Lauren Long, Colin Lynch, Shyam Mani, Greg McGee, Iva Milo, Nondini Naqui, Mark Newberg, Rachel O'Neil, Sue Pfeffer, Ethan Pierce, Patrick Quinton-Brown, Nevin Raj, Sasha Ramani, Gustavo Resendiz Jr., David Su, Patrick Trisna, Dianne Twombly, Christopher Usih, Rohan Wadhwa, Naicheng

Wangyu, Soo Wong, Peter Xu, Noah Yonack, Harry Yu, Ike Zhang, Richard Zhang, and Sandy Zhu.

For the advice, anecdotes, feedback, introductions, and support—and for dealing with my constant pitches—I thank my HBS Section I "Iguana Samura-Is" and the HBS founder community: Daniel Abrams, Michael Aft, Wade Anderson, Jonathan Arena, Jeremy Au, Ward Ault, Graham Ballbach, Wills Begor, Robby Berner, Elizabeth Blake, Gonzalo Boada Giménez, Grant Boren, Sophia Brañes, Jessie Cai, Allison Campbell, Laura Carpenter, Henry Cashin, Eric Chavez, Fay Chen, Stephanie Cheng, Sooah Cho, Spencer Christensen, Michael Clancy, Christianna Coltart, Mike Contillo, Gabe Cunningham, Katherine Degnen, Matt Delaney, Felipe Delgado, Sahil Dewan, Bahia El Oddi, Carolyn Fallert, Deeni Fatiha, Vicente Fauro, Javier Fernandez, Michi Ferreol, Quinn Fitzgerald, Brandon Freiberg, Lily Fu, Francesca Furchtgott, Juan David Galindo, Matt Graham, Rashard Green, Shray Gulati, Natalie J. Guo, Michael Haddad, Daniel Handlin, Benjamin Hardy, Christopher Henry, Marc Howland, Kristina Hristova, Linda Huynh, Sander Intelmann, Hari Iyer, Nancy Jin, Ashwini Kadaba, Ryan Karmouta, Salima Kassam, Ananth Kasturiraman, Irene Keskinen, Reilly Kiernan, David Kim, Julia Klimaszewska, Andrew Knez, Rafi Kohlberg, Evan Kornbluh, Aditi Kumar, Ben Lacey, Hans Latta, Catherine Lee, Brian Levin, Jenna Levy, Kenny Lim, Rachel Lipson, Beijun Luo, Alison MacLeod, Amrita Mainthia, Yarden Maoz, Fredrik Marø, Peggy Mativo-Ochola, David Mbau, Elise McDonald, Pat McMann, Amit Megiddo, Anita Mehrotra, Michael Mekeel, Shantanu Misra, Deviyani Misra-Godwin, Roberto Morfino, Rahkeem Morris, Stanislav Moskovtsev, Josefin Muehlbauer, Patrick Nealon, Clarisse Neu, Benjamin Newmark, Grace Ng, Erika Ohashi, Sonja Page, Sanchali Pal, Sam Palmisano, Iryna Papalamava, Apoorva Pasricha, Saurav Patyal, Ana Pedrajo, Phoebe Peronto, Amira Polack, Olivier Porté, Shveta Raina, Krishna Rajendran, JJ Raynor, Michael Reslinski, Misan Rewane, Hunter Richard, Caitlin Riederer, Ken Rowe, Ben Samuels, Tafadzwa Samushonga, Jose Sanchez, Beau Sangassapaviriya, Levana Sani, Michael Sard, Rebecca Scharfstein, Jon Schechter, Monty Sharma, Quinn Shelton, Mimi Sheng, Doug Shultz, Andrew Sierra, Denzil Sikka, Michael Silvestri, Kamoy Smalling, Taylor Spector, Sam Stone, Rohit Sudheendranath, Colleen Tapen, Stephen Temple, Liz Thomas, Pierre H. Thys, Tarunika Tolani, Stephanie Tong, Chad Trausch, Sujay Tyle, Saksham Uppal, Erika

Uyterhoeven, David Vakili, Sharif Vakili, Gustavo Vaz, Fangfang Wang, Dan Weisleder, Michael Alan Williams, Aaron Wirshba, Jon Wofsy, Maria Woodman, Lynn Xie, Catherine Xu, Shelly Xu, Takafumi Yamada, Jeremy Yan, Roland Yang, Nanako Yano, Ravi Yegya-Raman, Brian Yeh, Angelo Zegna, Yujie Zeng, Mary Zhang, and Itamar Zur.

For all the thought-provoking discussions, personal anecdotes, and encouragement, I thank members of the Boston Shapers, including Ryan Ansin, Johan Bjurman Bergman, Sean J. Cheng, Howard Cohen, Giffin Daughtridge, Anand Ganjam, Juan Giraldo, Kyle Gross, Neekta Hamidi, Rachel Kanter, Tanveer Kathawalla, Millie Liu, Phil Michaels, David Mou, Ryan O'Malley, Josuel Plasencia, Abhishek Raman, Michael Raspuzzi, Jake Reisch, Jen Riedel, Meicen Sun, Yannis K. Valtis, and Bozhanka Vitanova.

For helping me appreciate the challenging but rewarding work of advising students who don't know what they don't know, I thank my colleagues at UMass Boston, including Jennifer Barone, William Farrick, Deborah Federico, Adesuwa Igbineweka, Mark Kenyon, Michael Mahan, Katherine Newman, Matthew Power-Koch, and Amanda Stupakevich, and the Adams House tutor corps and First-Gen, Low-Income and Career Advising teams, including Varnel Antoine, Ceylon Auguste-Nelson, Matt Burke, Jerren Chang, Marina Connelly, Medha Gargeya, Sheila Gholkar, Jelani Hayes, Shandra Jones, Shannon Jones, Amber Kuzmick, John Muresianu, Rumbi Mushavi, Emma Ogiemwanye, Dennis Ojogho, Judith Palfrey, Sean Palfrey, Sunny Patel, Osiris Rankin, Kathryn C. Reed, Weilu Shen, Timothy Smith, Aubry Threlkeld, Emiliano Valle, and Larissa Zhou.

For embracing my minimal-viable-product pitches, offering early feedback, and extending opportunities to field-test my ideas, I thank Brian Bar, Diana Chien, Justin Kang, Paul Martin, Amanda Sharick, Karen Shih, and Andrew Yang.

For the extra couch and the midnight stroll through the streets of Shanghai that inspired this whole journey, I thank Chris Royle and Andrew Yoo.

For the (literal) long walks on the beach that sparked my journey down the path less traveled, I thank H. Wook Kim.

For their insights, mentorship, and guidance, I thank the faculty and staff of HBS, many of whom took the time to meet with someone they had never even taught before, including Ethan Bernstein, Ryan Buell, Jeff Bussgang, Timothy Butler, Clayton Christensen, Michael Chu, Thomas DeLong, Amy Edmondson, Kristin Fabbe, Kristen Fitzpatrick, David Fubini, Joseph Fuller, Jodi Gernon, Shikhar Ghosh, Lena Goldberg, Paul Gompers, Boris Groysberg, Jonas Heese, Laura Huang, Chet Huber, Robert Huckman, Elizabeth Keenan, William Kerr, John J-H Kim, Rembrand Koning, Mark Kramer, Christopher Malloy, Tony Mayo, Ramana Nanda, Mark Roberge, Richard Ruback, Amy Schulman, Willy Shih, Lou Shipley, Erik Stafford, Brian Trelstad, Ashley Whillans, and Royce Yudkoff.

Last but not least, I thank the countless individuals who didn't fit neatly into any of the categories above but whose anecdotes and insights led to this book. Many of these individuals answered my cold emails, endured my relentless probing, and shared candid reflections that became the basis of this book. I have used some of these individuals' names as pseudonyms for the real protagonists in this book as a gesture of gratitude (and to preserve the anonymity of the actual person). Among this group are individuals such as Andrea Abbott, Asset Abdualiyev, CJ Abeleda, Rabia Abrar, Susan Acton, Kristen Adamowski, Ehizogie Marymartha Agbonlahor, Muhammad Khisal Ahmed, Shirley Ai, Bob Allard, Lindsay Alperin, Verenice Andrade, Olivia Angiuli, Carl Arnold, Sare' Arnold, Jeremy Aronson, Casey Arrington, Christina Asadorian, Sasanka Atapattu, Afnan Attia, Andrea Bachyrycz, Shota Bagaturia, Ally Baldwin, Somya Banwari, Jon Barrett, Ryan Batter, Yonas Bayu, Julie Belben, Amy Benoit, Anthony Benoit, Steven J. Berger, Saba Beridze, Thomas Bernhardt-Lanier, Julee Bertsch, Mehnaaz Bholat, Maxwell Bigman, Sarah Bishop, Nicolas Blanco-Galindo, Robert Blank, Katie Bollbach, Steve Bonner, Leopold Bottinger, Maria Camila Brango, Nick Breedlove, Beth Brettschneider, Don Brezinski, Neil Bronfin, Ben Brooks, David Bryan, Pamela Campbell, Tobias Campos, Evan Cao, Deb Carroll, Jocelyn Carter, Sarah Case, Clarice Chan, Leila Chan Currie, Alexandria Chase, Brad Chattergoon, Min Che, Kevin Chen, Nina Chen, Luke Cheng, Jonah Chevrier, Prasidh Chhabria, Althea Chia, Nathan Chin, Kao Zi Chong, Adam Chu, Eric Chung, Cindy Churchill, Priscilla Claman, Tom Clay, Sam Clemens, Keith Cline, Celine Coggins, Chris Colbert, Emmet Colbert, Miles Collyer, Michael Concepcion, Susan Connor, Sarah Connors, Giovanni Conserva, Ashley

Cooke, Kerry Whorton Cooper, Kailani Cordell, Ben Cornish, Ryan Craig, Albert Cui, Jake Cui, Matthew Curry, Taylor Dallin, Annie Dang, Francesco Daniele, Samuel Daviau, Graham Davis, Ryan Davis, Daniel Debow, Gwendolyn Delgado, Shaan Desai, Mike Dezube, Alice Diamond, Caitlin DiMartino, Jake Dinerman, Amanda Dobbie, Omer Dobrescu, Brian Doyle, Connor Doyle, Tom Dretler, Thomas Dunleavy, Anne Dwane, Thanushi Eagalle, Brendan Eappen, Oliver Edmond, Dena Elkhatib, Bashir Elmegaryaf, Mary Elms, Olivia Engellau, Andrea Esposito, Kayla Evans, Ronny Fang, Zev Farber, Awais Farooq, Caroline Fay, Josh Feinberg, Leslie Feingerts, Dave Ferguson, Benji Fernandes, Jessica Flores, Shannon Flynn, Alexandra Foote, Abby Forbes, Aoife Fortin, Aisha Francis, Debra Franke, David Frankel, Julia Freeland Fisher, Nathan Fry, Olivia Fu, Cheng Gao, Jack Gao, Andrew Garcia, Valeria Garcia, Andres Garcia Lopez, Gerry Garvin, Joan Gass, Bob Gatewood, Rachel Gibson, Francine Gierak, Ali Gitomer, Katerina Glyptis, Rob Go, Diana Godfrey, Irvin Gómez, Andre Gonthier, Andre Gonzalez, Dan Gonzalez, Josh Gottlieb, Raffi Grinberg, Cindy Guan, Matthew Guidarelli, Lucy Guo, Deanna Gutierrez, Guillermo Samuel Hamlin, Longzhen Han, Crystel Harris, Emma Harrison-Trainor, Najib Hayat, Seamus Heaney, Tyler Hester, Mark Hoeplinger, Stephen Hong, Junaid Hoosen, Daniel Horgan, Eddie Horgan, Will Houghteling, Alice Hsiung, Eric Huang, Yingzi Sakura Huang, Alisha Hudani, Matt Hui, Michael Huntley, Urooj Hussain, Ian Ingles, Kathleen Jarman, Chetan Jhaveri, Alysha Johnson Williams, Saumya Joshi, Sarah June, Rick Kamal, Yinan Kang, Howard Kaplan, Imane Karroumi, Lance Katigbak, Nilu Kazemi, Marie Keil, Julia Kemp, Iqra Khan, Qasim Khan, Jaymin Kim, Cheryl Kiser, Lisa Kleitz, Carin-Isabel Knoop, Nathaniel Koloc, Jocelyn Krauss, Carl Kreitzberg, Claudia Krimsky, Andy Ku, Kara Kubarych, Justin Kulla, Ruth Kwakwa, Adrian Kwok, Scott LaChapelle, Margot Lafrance, Debbie Lai, Kriti Lall, Clement Lam, Michelle LaRoche, Heidi Larson, Atoor Lawandow, Fran Lawler, Leslie Laws, Tuongvan Le, Ryan Leaf, Antina Lee, Claire Lee, Trevor Lee, Zhihan Lee, James Leeper, Jolene Lehr, John Leung, Aner Levkovich, Linda Lewi, Junyi Li, Mary Li, Yuanjian Carla Li, Kevin Liang, Sandy Liang, Rachel Liddell, Bill Lin, Jessica Lin, Elizabeth Ling, John Liu, Tina Liu, Jake Livengood, Daniel Lobo, Vrinda Loiwal, Brian Longmire, Laura Thompson Love, Nicholas

Lowell, Helen Lu, Yin Lu, Gina Lucente-Cole, Kory Lundberg, Kelly Luo, Ande Lyons, Shannon Lytle, David Ma, Marco Ma, Ruby Maa, Ary Maharaj, Fazlur Malik, Bill Manley, Lyn Martin, Brian Matt, Linley McConnell, Karen McCrank, Metta McGarvey, Tessie McGough, Noelle McIsaac, Eleanor Meegoda, Rishab Mehan, Bill Mei, Emily Meland, Rui Meleiro, Michelle Mendes-Swidzinski, Christina Mendez, Jesse Mermell, Matt Meyersohn, Kyle Miller, Fatima Mohammad, Catherine Money, David Moon, Brian Morgan, Eric Morris, Madeleine Mortimore, Robin Mount, Thomas Murphy, Kennan Murphy-Sierra, Brian Mwarania, Annie Nam, Anthony Nardini, Katie Ng-Mak, Dina Nguyen, Kristine Nguyen, Patrick Nihill, Tasnoba Nusrat, Claire O'Connell, Tom O'Reilly, Lia O'Donnell, Ben Ohno, Chiderah Okoye, Ana Olano, Justin Ossola, Eric Ouyang, Scott Overdyke, Natalie Owen, Kayode Owens, Laiza Padilla, James Palano, Aaron Palmer, Ben Palmer, Belinda Pang, Rohan Parakh, Santiago Pardo Sánchez, Nisha Parikh, Christie Park, Hannah Park, Linda Passarelli, Priya Patel, Zeel Patel, India Peek Jensen, Kristine Pender, Angie Peng, Sally Pennell, Maren Peterson, Sharon Peyer, Steve Pfrenzinger, Alex Pham, Tyler Piazza, Jules Pieri, Ruben Pinchanski, Dan Pinnolis, Deeneaus Polk, Andi Pollinger, Iva Poppa, Emma Potvin, Ian Pu, Siya Raj Purohit, Katherine Qian, Andrew Quinn, Angela Quitadamo, Katie Rae, Aaliyah Rainey, Saketh Rama, Manjari Raman, Andrés Ramírez Cardona, Sherwet Rashed, Anuv Ratan, Cate Reavis, Rachel Redmond, Tristian Reid, Sheila Reindl, Nini Ren, Alexander Rendon, Brian Reynolds, Lori Richardson, Lynne Richardson, Andrea Rickey, Paul Riley, Adriana Rivas, Stever Robbins, Jabril Robinson, Maria Rodmell, Joan Ronayne, Tanya Rosbash, Brad Rosen, Arielle Rothman, Izzy Rubin, Maria Ruiz, Ali Saddiq, Ahmad Jawed Sakhi, Roland Salatino, Juaquin Sanchez, Shelby Sandhu, Marilyn Santiesteban, Steve Schewe, Peter Schirripa, Rosalie Schraut, Amna Shaikh, Ali Sharif, Kush Sharma, Emily Shen, Courtney Sherman, Ayane Shiga, Erin Shortell, Amanda Shuey, Jane Shui, Stuti Shukla, Jesse Shulman, María Sigüenza, Zoe Silverman, Christian Simoy, Samuel Singer, Navjeet Singh, Hirsh Sisodia, Alvin Siu, Erik Skantze, Michael Skok, Fran Slutsky, Arman Smigielski, Alexis Smith, Debbie Smith, Fraser Smith, Marta Sobur, Daniela Spagnuolo, Jonathan Sparling, Sunil Sreekanth, Rahul Srinivasan, Vish Srivastava, Caitlin Stanton, Julia Starr, Stephanie Steele, Terry Sterling, Beverley Stevens,

Heather Stevenson, Grace Strong, Avinaash Subramaniam, Kent Summers, Edward Sun, Jake Sussman, Theodore Sutherland, Matthew Sutton, Paul Syta, Thomas Taft, Karis Tai, Selena Tan, Audrey Tao, Amy Taul, Chris Taylor, Ryan Tencer, Tyler Terriault, Tracy Terry, Sarah Tesar, Matthew Thomas, Susan Thomas, Kevin Thompson, Jerry Ting, Emma Toh, Michael Trang, Seth Trudeau, David Tsui, Marianna Tu, Matt Tucker, Matt Turzo, Jocelyn Tuttle, Katie Urban, Michael Uy, Amira Valliani, Amy Van Kirk, Cynthia King Vance, James Vander Hooven, Olga Vasileva, David Vencis, Daniela Vera, Claudia Villanueva, Tomas Vita, Triet Vo, Claire Wadlington, Wajieha Waheed, Alyson Wall, Katie Walsh, Annie Wang, Lisa Wang, Marilyn Wang, Michele Wang, Ray Ruichen Wang, RunLin Wang, Susan Wang, Yutong Wang, Tom Ward, Nessim Watson, Anaëlle Pema Weber, Carolina Weber, Howard Wei, Joanne Weiss, Kara Weiss, Scott Westfahl, Daniel Wexler, Megan White, Gabriel Sylvester Wildberger, Tara Wilson, Jason Winmill, Basuki Winoto, Alexis Wolfer, Felix Wong, Matthew Wozny, Allison Wu, Bryan Wu, Dan Wu, Irene Wu, Yifan Wu, Wentao Xiong, Anita Xu, George Xu, Nicolas Xu, Vicky Xu, BerBer Xue, Jonathan Yam, Cha Cha Yang, Cherry Yang, Isabel Yishu Yang, Julie Yen, Jennifer Yoon, Grace Young, Serene Yu, Kevin Yuen, Charlie Zhang, Danny Zhang, Linda Zhang, Peiyi Zhang, Lili Zhao, Selena Zhao, Lucy Zhong, Chris Zhou, Muhammed Ziauddin, Lara Zimmerman, Lillian Zuo, and David Zylberberg. (To anyone I forgot, *thank you*. My oversight reflects my forgetfulness rather than my lack of gratitude. Please get in touch. I owe you a drink.)

And to all the people who paid it forward to the people above—and who, in turn, made this work possible—know that you too are a part of this relay race. Thank you for your work. Please keep doing what you're doing.

ABOUT THE AUTHOR

GORICK NG is a career adviser at Harvard, specializing in coaching first-generation, low-income students. He is also a researcher with the Managing the Future of Work project at Harvard Business School. Ng has worked in career services at the University of Massachusetts Boston, management consulting at the Boston Consulting Group (BCG), investment banking at Credit Suisse, and education policy at the Toronto District School Board. He was named one of *Time* magazine's top 25 future leaders from around the world and has also been featured in the *Toronto Star*, the *Globe and Mail*, the *New York Post*, *World Journal*, and on CBC. Ng serves on the board of directors of the Toronto Foundation for Student Success and is a member of the World Economic Forum Global Shapers Community. Ng, a first-generation college student, is a graduate of Harvard College and Harvard Business School. Find him at gorick.com.